THEY CALLED HER
RECKLESS

Also By Janet Barrett

On The Fence: A Parent's Handbook
of Horseback Riding

THEY CALLED HER
RECKLESS

A TRUE STORY OF WAR, LOVE AND
ONE EXTRAORDINARY HORSE

U U U

JANET BARRETT

Tall Cedar Books
Chester, CT

First Printing, 2013.
Second Printing, 2014.

Paperback ISBN 978-0-9898040-0-4

Cover Design: Sandy C. Vaccaro
Interior Design: Marilena Vaccaro

Tall Cedar Books
36 Goose Hill Road
Chester, CT 06412

www.rapages.net/jbarrett/

About_Reckless@comcast.net

To my husband,
Walter Terlecki,

and

To all those who knew
and loved Reckless,
without whose help this book
could not have been written.

CONTENTS

One   A Racehorse Joins The Marines *1*

Two   The New Recruit *29*

Three   On The Line *55*

Four   One Extraordinary Horse *81*

Five   Wrapping Up The War *97*

Six   Sergeant Reckless, Ma'am *115*

Seven   California Here She Comes *133*

Eight   Another New Life *149*

Epilogue *165*

Notes And Sources *169*

Acknowledgments *173*

About The Author *175*

Notes On Production *177*

Chapter One

A RACEHORSE JOINS THE MARINES

—— 1 ——

UShe rolled through the front gate, nimbly balancing herself in an open box trailer. Up front, the Marines riding in the jeep were patently nonchalant as they returned the guard's salute. Behind them was hitched one of those little two-wheel trailers, so small that its passenger had to stand cattycorner to fit in at all. The wooden slats they had stuck upright on either side provided some support, they hoped, as the rig bounced along the rough, dirt and gravel road that ran north from Seoul to where the 75ers and the Tankers were in reserve camp.

The two groups weren't together very often, only when the Fifth Regiment rotated off the front line, and that would be over in a few more days. It was early October 1952, daily temperatures already dipping to the mid-40s in that pocket of land called the Western Sector. This day, however, was a pleasant exception—nice enough for the guys to grab a pick-up game of softball which, in the late afternoon, was still ongoing just inside the camp entrance. Suddenly, Sergeant Chuck Batherson looked up and groaned audibly, "What the hell? Now I've seen everything." It ended the game, the batting order and the score quickly forgotten as everyone turned toward the new arrival.

Steadily gazing back at those crowding around the rig was a very small horse, not a miniature, mind you, but one no bigger than a medium-sized pony. She was red—called sorrel in the West, chestnut elsewhere. Her pretty, chiseled head, long mane, and white blaze down the center of her nose were matched, as those peering over the sides of the trailer could see, by slender legs, three of which had white stockings. The contradiction was that the elegant head and legs joined one surprisingly sturdy body— well-muscled shoulders, a strong back, and a broad rump. Or as Rogers and Hammerstein wrote in *South Pacific*, their hit musical of the time, about another dame, "She was broad where a broad should be broad." This "dame" was also clearly unfazed by the growing commotion.

"C'mon, you two, let's figure out how we're going to get her out of this thing," prodded Lieutenant Eric Pedersen, commanding officer of the 75ers, climbing out of the jeep ahead of the others. With the Fifth Regiment in reserve since mid-September, there had been a little more time to get his plan underway—and right now that meant getting his four-legged charge settled. Still, he was quietly enjoying the reaction around him.

The trailer was a solid box and getting even a small horse out took some maneuvering. Inching the rig down a slight incline, they positioned it with the rear lip of the box even with the higher ground. Gently coaxing, they turned their passenger around so that she faced the back, and she stepped up and onto solid ground with ease. At three years old, or maybe four, so Pedersen had been told, she seemed accommodating and comfortable being handled by her new owners.

The Marines, done with the day's activities and ready for chow, were immediately taken with this little horse in their midst. "Nobody had any idea," said Batherson. "Yeah, all of a sudden, here's this horse." Whatever she was doing there, she was easily the best diversion of the day. A noisy bunch kept up the questioning:

"Where'd she come from?"

"Is she ours? We going to keep her?"

"Why'd you get her?"

"She's cute. What's her name?" And on and on.

"Hold it, hold it. Simmer down," chuckled Pedersen. "Meet your new ammo carrier." Stroking her neck as he eyed his men, he asked, "So, what do you think? Who's got a good name?" Almost in unison came back:

"How about Reckless?"

"Yeah, you got it. Reckless."

"Sure, that's us. Reckless."

It was decided. An apt choice, at that, since Pedersen was in charge of the 75mm Recoilless Rifle Platoon, better known as the Reckless Rifles. The platoon was part of the Anti-Tank Company of the U.S. Marine Corps Fifth Regiment. Spontaneously, someone passed a hat around and the guys started a collection to help pay for her keep. "I threw in ten bucks," said Batherson. "True, she was going to be the 75ers' horse and not ours. But so what? What the hell was I going to do with the money over there?"

Besides, Batherson had ridden horses a lot as a teenager and her presence, while startling, no doubt offered a certain comfort level. At age 19, he had already been in Korea a year and, like so many recruits, he made no bones about his rush to get there. Raised in Detroit, Michigan, he joined the Marine Corps two weeks after high school graduation. "We had a big beer party at the lake. You know, all the girls and all the guys. Then I left and didn't come back for almost three years," he recalled.

At this point, Pedersen was hollering over the ruckus, "Hey, Gunny, meet your new charge." A half smile on his face, he was looking straight at Gunnery Sergeant Joseph Latham, who was already striding toward the crowd. Reckless, seemingly at ease in the midst of the goings on, was watching, too. Likely, it was the same calm look, the steadiness, that had attracted Pedersen earlier that day.

They had driven out at dawn, Pedersen and the two he had quietly tapped to come with him, Corporal Philip Carter and Scout Sergeant Willard Berry. The camp where the regiment was in reserve was a big, sprawling place, north of the Imjin River but still several miles back from the front line. Traffic in the compound was commonplace—visitors coming in and out, daily deliveries from the big Marine supply depots—and no one batted an eye as the three took off, pulling the small, utility trailer behind their jeep. Like a lot of American military equipment in Korea, the trailer was probably a World War II model. Most of them were made by one of two companies, the American Bantam Car Company, of Butler, Pennsylvania, the first to invent and build jeeps, in 1940, or the Willys-Overland Motor Company, of Toledo, Ohio. Utility was the operative word for these tough, watertight boxes. Four feet wide by six feet long and mounted on two large hooded wheels, they hauled cargo over land or on water. Still, a horse—that was unusual.

By all accounts or, more precisely, the lack of them, the plan to acquire a horse had been kept under wraps. Pedersen had run his idea by the Fifth Regiment's First Battalion Commander, Lieutenant Colonel Alexander Gentleman, and found him supportive. Captain Henry Checklou, Commander of the Regiment's Anti-Tank Company, though less enthused still gave a nod and passed it on. Moving up the chain of command and gathering assorted okays as it went, the proposal remained a green-lighted secret. It was a safe bet, however, that Joe Latham also knew what was about to unfold, but as closed-mouthed as Pedersen, he never let on.

Pedersen's reason for wanting a horse had crystallized over the previous few months. It was simple, really. The men of the Recoilless Rifle Platoon needed help hauling ammunition up the steep hills of Korea, a terrain that, as it climbed, was virtually beyond the reach of trucks. It required grunt work, and Pedersen had watched how backbreaking it was, bringing the 20- to 23-pound shells up to the gun positions. Each shell was in a cardboard sleeve, making the package about two feet long, and it had to be carried that way and not unpacked until the shell was about to be used.

This was not just heavy, cumbersome work, but the men had to make repeated trips up and down the hills, sometimes for hours on end. Each fire mission (a planned gun fight) had basic differences like the amount of ammunition that would be available, and the type of terrain where they would be fighting. Trucks transported the shells from Headquarters Company, at the rear of forward camp, driving as close as possible but stopping behind the reach of incoming enemy fire. Usually, between there and the hill to be climbed was a rice paddy, ruined by war but still boggy enough to trap a truck trying to get across. Beyond the paddy came the ascent to the ridgeline along a winding, craggy footpath.

Most guys could handle two shells, one laid crosswise on each shoulder, in addition to the other gear they carried. That in itself amounted to 60 pounds or more of water, food, small arms and ammunition, survival gear, flashlight, batteries, medical kit, and an all-important change of socks, plus the helmet, flak jacket, and clothing that each man wore. Some found it helpful to use a canvas backpack with deep pockets that held the long tubes vertically. Either way, for most, no matter how they carried them, two shells were the limit, and only a really big man could manage three. The standout memory was of Private First Class Monroe Coleman, a strapping, six-foot-plus Marine from Loa, Utah. It must have been a sight to behold because everyone described it the same way: Coleman, with his own gear strapped to his back, steadying a cardboard wrapped shell across each shoulder, then stooping low enough for someone to position a third across the other two, close to the back of Coleman's head. Grabbing the ends of the perpendicular tubes with both hands, and hoisting at least 130 pounds on his upper body, he would straighten up and stride out.

"He was a young kid," chuckled Guy Wagoner, from North Carolina, "but then we were all young kids in Korea. I turned 21 there, and they called me an old man." Age 18 and eager when he enlisted in the Marine Corps in Baltimore, Maryland, Wagoner told the recruiter he could leave "any old time," though admitted he didn't expect to hear it would be the same day. It was the last day of January 1950, and he pointed out, "I made his quota for the month." With ordnance as his job specialty, Wagoner was slated to attend school at Marine Corps Base Quantico in Virginia, but the abrupt start of the Korean War changed many orders, his included. Before long he was on his way to Camp Pendleton, and then to Korea in early 1952. Assigned to the Fifth Regiment, then up in the mountains on the Eastern Front, the vicious cold of that first winter left an indelible impression on Wagoner. "The wind came down out of Manchuria. Our dungarees were about the same thickness as you'll find today, and we had two sets of long underwear, tops and bottoms. That was all the protection we had from the wind. I've never been so cold in my life," he said. Better winter gear arrived eventually and made a big difference, but that harsh first memory of Korea never left him.

—— **2** ——

Wagoner was in the 13th draft, the last of what was called "the push" —still that phase of the war when the combatants were on the move, attacking and being attacked. The Marines did not have a draft in the usual sense, but used the term within the Corps for guys being sent to Korea. By the time Wagoner got there, the war was a year and a half old, and a conflict that neither side ever expected to develop had already exacted a terrible toll. Americans were back in a part of the world they had left only a few short years before, at the end of World War II, in a country that had quickly gone from limited international interest to front-page news around the world.

No matter where they went through boot camp, most Marine recruits wound up at Camp Pendleton, their final stop before sailing from San Diego on one of the many ships taking troops and cargo to and from Korea. The newly established Military Sea Transportation Service grew to a fleet of several hundred, mostly commercial U.S. merchant marine ships, plus ships from the National Defense Reserve Fleet and more than a hundred World War II Victory ships. Crossings were generally an unpleasant introduction to what lay ahead: depending on the ship, as many as 5,000 men jammed aboard for three weeks, sleeping in hammocks four deep in the hold, where everything else went on, as well. When ships hit rough seas, predictably life in the hold turned foul.

Wagoner's ship was one of the unlucky ones. When it hit a typhoon, he recalled, "the bow went up so high, you'd have had room to drive a truck across the water under it. The propeller would come out of the water and the whole ship would shudder. Then the bow would crash down and we were awash. We had about 3,800 men on board and almost everybody was sick." Asked how many days he was at sea, he replied, "way too many."

Ships landed at Inchon, then troops moved on to Ascom City, home of the huge Marine Replacement and Supply Depot on adjacent Kimpo Peninsula. The site had changed hands twice before. First built for use by the Japanese military during their occupation of Korea, it was also used post World War II by the U.S. Army. Some of the buildings came from the Japanese; "Ascom" came from Army Support Command, the short form for the U.S. Eighth Army's Logistics Installation. It was a transfer point for arriving and departing Marines, and they were billeted there until further transportation was ready. Guys heading for the front picked up a rattling old train to the railhead at Munsan-ni, then were trucked the rest of the way to their units.

The situation in Korea had actually unfolded over many years, not surprisingly long before anyone beyond that country and its immediate neighbors had any understanding of what was happening. But as World War II drew to a close, and the surrender of Japan was imminent, the U.S. and its Allies realized that a new scenario was taking shape: Korea, annexed by Japan since 1910, after the close of the Russo-Japanese War, would soon be liberated. People who had chafed under their occupier's authority for 35 years were poised to reclaim their country. And simmering ideologies—nationalism in the South, led by Syngman Rhee, and communism in the North, championed by Kim Il-sung—were on a collision course. The U.S. and its Allies realized what could happen and jointly voiced concern for Korea's future.

Korea had never been of much strategic interest to the U.S. By late in the war, however, Presidents Roosevelt and, later, Truman, along with British Prime Minister Churchill, and Soviet Premier Stalin agreed that a plan of action was necessary. The decision was to make the country a trusteeship, administered by the United States-Soviet Union Joint Commission. This arrangement was to last five years, after which Korea would be independent. In fact, Korean pressure ended the trusteeship in three years.

In August 1945, the Allies agreed with Russia's plan to declare war against Japan and send troops into Manchuria and North Korea. Uneasy that Russia really planned to take control of the entire Korean Peninsula, the U.S. transferred a small contingent of Army troops, under the command of Major General John R. Hodge, from Okinawa to South Korea. To further secure the situation, the U.S. divided the peninsula along the 38th Parallel. The move was supported by the Allies and officially created the two Koreas. Russia never sent troops into the South, as the U.S. feared. At the end of World War II, Russia accepted the Japanese surrender in North Korea and the U.S. accepted it in South Korea.

Through 35 years of Japanese occupation, Koreans saw the fabric of their lives obliterated as piece by piece, Japan methodically replaced Korea's government, educational system, culture, and language with its own. Post war, the prospect of outside powers controlling Korea again was unthinkable and civil unrest spread quickly. The U.S. stabilized the situation but there was little impetus or budget to do much more.

Humanitarian and strategic efforts on the part of the U.S. were focused primarily on Europe, helping countries devastated by years of war to rebuild. As the most powerful member of the newly created North Atlantic Treaty Organization, the U.S. was most concerned with Europe's defense, particularly in light of Russia's developing sphere of control in Eastern Europe. So many of our resources were channeled westward that President Truman recommended withdrawing troops from both Koreas and turning their problems over to the United Nations.

The U.N. accepted and began pressing both sides to hold free elections by May 1948. This the South did, creating a National Assembly and, over the next two months, producing a constitution and electing 73-year-old Syngman Rhee as president of the new Republic of Korea. The North spurned the elections and dismissed the results, then in September formed the Democratic People's Republic of Korea lead by 36-year-old Kim Il-sung. North Korea also claimed jurisdiction over all Korea, South and North.

In September 1948, the trusteeship ended. The U.S. and Russia withdrew their forces from the peninsula, and Korea was a free nation. Each side left behind assorted equipment, far more from Russia for

North Korea than the U.S. gave to the South. By late 1949, talk of a North Korean invasion was commonplace, but the U.S. ignored it. Outwardly, both Koreas pressed for reunification while, covertly, increased cross-border probes, skirmishes, and outright border attacks inflamed the atmosphere well into 1950.

On June 25, the curtain came down on whatever hopes still existed to unify the two countries when the North invaded the South, sending troops and tanks across the breadth of the 38th Parallel. Quickly, the United Nations Security Council passed two resolutions: that same day, requesting North Korea to cease hostilities and withdraw its forces to the 38th Parallel, and on June 27, asking member nations to come to South Korea's aid in repelling the invader. Presumably, Russia would have opposed the resolutions, but its delegation was boycotting the council over the United Nation's support of Chiang Kai-Shek's government on Taiwan instead of Mao Zedong's regime in Communist China.

The main attack from the North came through the Uijongbu Corridor, a broad valley and the ancient southern route to Seoul. The capital fell to the enemy the next day, June 28.

—————— 3 ——————

It was always called a war—the Korean *War*—although President Truman sought to downplay it with the much less inciting title of Police Action—officially, a United Nations Police Action since it was under the control of the new United Nations. It started out badly, a mismatch of strengths, with the early advantage in North Korea's favor.

More striking was the extent to which all sides misjudged the situation—North Korea, China, and Russia believed the U.S. would not come to South Korea's aid and risk getting involved in another conflict so soon after World War II. The U.S. didn't think North Korea would invade and, later, badly miscalculated how involved China would get. None of the opponents anticipated the strength of the United Nation's commitment. The South Koreans saw most clearly what was coming in the year before war broke out, but even they had become inured to the volatility of the situation—and many were slow to believe that the June 25 attack was "the real one."

Post war, both sides were building their military strength, except that with the active participation of the Russians, North Korea was putting together an army far more formidable than that in the South. Syngman Rhee's pleas for U.S. assistance fell on deaf ears. The U.S. was willing to help South Korea get on its feet, hold elections, and form a government, but that would be the extent of the involvement. However, faced with the possibility that both Koreas could fall to the Communists and threaten the other countries in the region, President Truman backed the U.N. Security Council's decision to send forces in support of South Korea. North Korea's breach of the 38th Parallel, he believed, was aggression that must be stopped. He also hoped that committing naval and air support would suffice, and American ground troops would not be needed.

Almost immediately, it was apparent that an air and sea defense would not be enough. In the South, the Republic of Korea forces (ROK forces) totaled 98,000 (65,000 combat and 33,000 support troops) plus a paltry air force and no tanks, and they were desperately outnumbered. Opposing them were North Korean ground forces estimated to be anywhere from 150,000 to 200,000 (with another probable 30,000 in reserve) organized into ten infantry divisions, plus tanks and considerably more air power than in the South. Many ROK troops deserted or defected to the North. Those who stayed to fight were pushed down the peninsula, their retreat complicated by hordes of civilians fleeing south.

However strongly South Koreans believed that their northern counterparts would actually invade the South, it was a scenario that the United States disregarded. Caught off guard when the invasion occurred, with only an occupation force of fewer than 500 soldiers in the country, the U.S. began moving in Army forces from Japan and Okinawa. General of the Army Douglas MacArthur, Supreme Commander for the Allied Powers, was quickly appointed by Truman as Commander of United Nation Forces. He had overseen the U.S. occupation of Japan since its surrender in August 1945. In Korea, he assumed command of the U.S.-led coalition of troops from U.N. member nations.

U.S. Eighth Army and ROK forces stopped the North Korean onslaught on August 3, 1950, some one hundred miles above the southern tip of the peninsula. The firewall, known as the Pusan Perimeter, buffered the vital Port of Pusan and saved South Korea from being completely overrun. At that point, the U.S. Marines joined the fight, sending ashore the first wave of the Fifth Regiment's First Provisional Marine Brigade.

Through August, U.N. troops fought fiercely to hold the perimeter, at the same time preparing for the launch of a counteroffensive. The British, the only ally with forces close at hand, sent their 1,600-member 27th Infantry Brigade and the U.S. continued to build its strength as quickly as it could. By the beginning of September the U.N. troops totaled 180,000. Over the next three years, 14 additional U.N. nations committed combat troops, five noncombatant nations provided medical units, and various members also supplied naval and air support.

It would be two more years before Reckless came into the picture, the unlikely recruit of the Fifth Regiment. What her wartime experience was before that happened is an open question, although it can be established with reasonable certainty that she was not in Seoul from the time the war began. She might have been in the south around Pusan, but even more likely, she was still on her island homeland off the tip of the Korean Peninsula. Much was to transpire before she met Lieutenant Pedersen that first week in October 1952.

————— **4** —————

The U.S. Marine Corps built itself back up to a wartime force with stunning speed. Budgetary cutbacks and personnel drawdowns had slashed the Corps to some 20 percent of its high-water mark of World War II, when more than 475,000 Marines swelled its ranks, the most in the Corps' history. Unlike President Roosevelt, President Truman was no fan of the Corps, calling them the Navy's police force and insisting that, as far as he was concerned, that is how they would remain. But the possible consequences of a North Korea-South Korea clash overrode his personal feelings. Moreover, MacArthur's experiences with the Marines in the Pacific Theater during World War II had convinced the general that the Marines were first rate and he wanted them in Korea, and fast.

The Marines pushed the envelope. Countering the opinion of the U.S. Joint Chiefs of Staff, who concluded that the Marine First Division could not be deployed before November or December, it arrived off the Korean coast, combat ready, on September 14, 1950. The next day, the Fifth Regiment came ashore at Wolmi-Do Island in the first move of MacArthur's brilliant and audacious invasion at Inchon, the port city for Seoul and the capital's access to the Yellow Sea. The brashness of his plan, code name Operation Chromite, also met with broad skepticism by the Joint Chiefs of Staff. The obstacles were many: Inchon's 32-foot tidal range, fierce currents, good enemy vantage points, and because Wolmi-Do had to be taken ahead of the main beachhead, no hope of tactical surprise. In addition, only on two days in September and one in October would the tides be high enough to give the big landing craft three hours ashore. MacArthur saw the negatives as a positive argument. The enemy would never expect such a risky attack, and certainly not in the short time it was organized.

MacArthur's instincts were correct. The invasion was a complete surprise and, it was widely agreed, his finest achievement of the war. Inchon also revalidated the U.S. Marine Corps in the eyes of its nation. The Fifth and First Regiments combined with Army forces as the X Corps, inflicted heavy casualties in seizing Kimpo Airfield, east of Inchon, then fought their way to Seoul. In bloody house-to-house combat, they wrested the heavily fortified city from the North Koreans. It was officially liberated on September 29, 1950 but, sadly, most of it was in ruins. Seoul would be the center of fighting twice more, when the North Koreans retook it in January 1951, and when U.N. forces liberated it again, this time permanently, two months after that.

Overall, it was an encouraging time. MacArthur's Inchon invasion and recapture of Seoul had broken the North Korean's lines and cut off their main supply routes, forcing them to retreat and wreaking havoc on their ability to fight the war. A second amphibious landing at Wonsan, on North Korea's east coast, set the stage for a push north by combined U.S. and ROK forces. They would sweep all the way to the Yalu River, North Korea's border with China and, it was expected, bring the war to a rapid close. Common talk among servicemen was that they would be home for Christmas.

Unfortunately, the military ignored one key factor: Communist China's repeated warnings to the U.N. that if North Korea was invaded they would enter the war. It was a costly mistake for all involved.

More than a quarter million Communist Chinese troops were massed along China's border with North Korea, and by the middle of fall 1950, units were pushing south. There were signs of trouble: ROK troops, the first to reach the Yalu River, took Chinese prisoners of war. Elsewhere military intelligence was also picking up indications of Chinese presence. Once the existence of Chinese forces in North Korea was confirmed, the numbers revealed were huge and their rapid involvement signaled the beginning of a much larger war. MacArthur's plan, to retake North Korea, the precursor to reuniting North and South, was no longer viable. In late November 1950, the Korean War escalated into what would become a protracted, ugly conflict that would not end until July 1953— more than two and a half years later.

Advancing north toward the Chosin Reservoir—the Eighth Army from the west and the Marines from the east—precipitated one of the worst battles of the war. Two hundred thousand Communist Chinese forced the Army to withdraw. The Marine Fifth and Seventh Regiments, surrounded by eight Chinese divisions, fought their way out in one of the epic battles of Marine history. The Marines were outnumbered eight to one by the Communist Chinese, and were forced to fight in the worst weather in 50 years: snow, wind, and temperatures as low as -40 degrees Fahrenheit. Losses on both sides were horrendous but the Chinese, whose express mission was to destroy the Marines, sustained far more casualties. With able men walking, the wounded and dead transported along with equipment, the Marines fought all the way to the port of Hungnam. Waiting there, an enormous armada evacuated troops and hordes of refugees. In a final salvo all port facilities were blown to oblivion.

Chosin elevated China's status as a military power, but the enemy's enormous losses ultimately ceded the edge to the U.N. forces. Major offensives would continue for another six months. Battles for Seoul were fought; the enemy again pushed down the peninsula, and U.N. troops forced them back into North Korea. Haltingly, peace talks began at Kaesong in July and fighting quieted down. By late summer, the talks stalled out and fighting once again heated up.

— 5 —

Americans never had much appetite for the war, and what little there was had dwindled. Korea was no longer a front-page story. Both sides knew the war was costing too much, in men and materiel, and it was time to find a way out. Truce talks resumed at Panmunjom in late October 1951, and a cease-fire line was drawn. It didn't please either side totally, and both sides would fight, literally, for adjustments. But going forward there was a new ground game.

The guys who showed up in Korea in the winter of 1951, and in the months thereafter, landed in a very different war. Positional warfare or trench warfare, it came down to the same thing—each side holding the territory that was theirs. U.N. forces fought against North Korea's attempts to seize additional land while looking for ways to adjust the line and make it more defendable. Combat ebbed and flowed, months of skirmishes and firefights escalated to entrenched, bloody battles—all of it filling time until the major powers could settle a war no one wanted in a way everyone would accept.

By early 1952, the combatants were essentially back where they had started, on either side of the 38th Parallel, the line that divided Korea into two countries after World War II. U.N. air forces commanded the skies over North and South, and naval forces had blockaded the entire coastline. Each side had their Main Line of Resistance (MLR), carved by miles and miles of deep trenches that snaked across the country. In these trenches, in fire holes and bunkers, and from behind ridges, the fight continued for the contested No Man's Land between the two main lines.

It was a battle for the area's major foothills, now designated Combat Outposts or simply Outposts, and losing them threatened each side's main line. The outposts were all numbered according to their height, and the Americans also named the most prominent among them after well-known faces and places: Hollywood pin-ups like Ava, Ginger, Hedy, Kate, Esther, Dagmar, Corrine, Ingrid, and Marilyn—although the latter supposedly was not for the famous Ms. Monroe, but for a hometown sweetheart—and places like Vegas, Reno, Carson, Bunker Hill, Detroit, Berlin and East Berlin.

In spring 1952, Lieutenant Eric Pedersen took command of the Fifth Regiment's Recoilless Rifle Platoon and within months solved a nagging problem in an innovative way. Sergeant John Moore, a Texas cowboy and one of the first to land in Korea with the First Provisional Marine Brigade, always thought Reckless exemplified what they told guys to do in combat.

"The Gunny Sergeant, he'd tell you that you weren't going to get everything you needed, and you were going to have to improvise. And I think she was a pretty good example of improvising," he said, chuckling. "Pedersen must have been a cowboy, or he knew something about horses."

Moore was right on both counts. Pedersen had grown up in Southern California and Jackson Hole, Wyoming. His paternal grandparents had been ranchers in several western states, finally around Jackson Hole, and at the family ranch, young Pedersen developed the love and affinity for horses that would stay with him through life. Years later in Korea, it made perfect sense to him that the right horse would help his Marines.

The characteristic most remembered by those who served under

Pedersen was how much he cared for his men. "He was that kind of person, always thinking of them first," said Guy Wagoner. "He loved his men, he looked out for them, and he expected a lot from them, too. He was number one, all the way." Most of the guys under him never really knew very much about him, though, a typical situation between officers and enlisted men. But those who served with him were glad they did, and those who got to Korea after he had rotated home wished they had met him.

At age 32, Pedersen was slim and angular, of medium height and upright bearing. He had a strong face with heavy eyebrows and, for the camera at least, a usually serious look. Wagoner's description of him as an enlisted man's officer had to have been rooted in his earlier years in the Corps. After enlisting in 1938, Private First Class Pedersen sailed on the USS Henderson between China and California, and on the USS Helena to South America. In 1942, he married Katherine Wells of San Diego, California. The couple met before Pedersen joined the Marines and, from the beginning, Mrs. Pedersen not only understood how important horses were to him, but she supported him fully.

Later that same year, Pedersen shipped out to the South Pacific. There he earned the title of "mustang," for someone who enters the service as an enlisted man and moves into the officer ranks, in his case to the rank of captain. As a battlefield promotion, however, the rank wasn't permanent, and did not accompany Pedersen when he was called back to Korea. Sergeant Wagoner shared many a beer with him—one of the few enlisted men to do so—and recalled Pedersen's bitterness at only being able to get the rank of second lieutenant upon returning to active duty. There was an ongoing rotation of troops in and out of Korea, and when new Marines showed up in the Recoilless Rifle Platoon, he would introduce himself at the next formation, saying:

"You can call me Pete. Or you can call me Mr. Pedersen. But the first sonofabitch who calls me 'Lieutenant Pedersen,' I'm going to slap his face."

Presumably everyone paid attention because no one recalled anyone ever getting slapped. Mostly they addressed him as Pete, said Wagoner, adding, "Pete was what I would call an old war dog, and a damn good one. He believed that if there was a war going on, he ought to be in it. He was that kind of person."

Pedersen and his father, John Douglas Pederson (Eric spelled his name as his grandfather had), provided an interesting counterpoint to the business of war. John Douglas was a small but important arms designer who worked for Remington and the U.S. government, and was held in high esteem by his peers. Indeed, none other than John Moses Browning, designer of the famed Browning Automatic Rifle, considered Pederson one of the finest designers ever.

The senior Pederson's most important designs were the 1918 Pederson Clip, a device that converted the 5-shot, bolt-action Springfield M1903 rifle to a semi-automatic rifle, and the Pedersen .276 semi-automatic rifle. Though the U.S. government was interested in both, each eventually was bypassed. The end of World War I stopped the forward track of the Pederson Clip. Then, after Pedersen worked on his .276-caliber rifle through much of the 1920s, the government eventually chose its competitor, the Garand M1 semi-automatic rifle, for mass production. Around 1930, Pedeson moved his family, his wife, Reata, son, Eric, and daughter, Kristi-Ray, to England and worked for the Vickers Company, that was also interested in his .276 rifle. After staying there for a couple of years, Pederson sent his family back to the U.S. He continued to work abroad with other governments into the mid-1930s, though none of his efforts led anywhere.

His son had already joined the Marines when the elder Pederson tried a last time to have one of his designs produced by the U.S. military. Through a company he formed in Michigan, he manufactured his M1 Carbine, again a competing design to the M1 Garand rifle. Unfortunately, ongoing difficulties undermined production and the U.S. government finally canceled his contract. Nonetheless, John Douglas Pederson continued to design, and when he died in 1951 he held about 90 patents. The perfect symmetry, that Eric would fire the rifle his father designed, never happened. The M1 Garand was still in use during the Korean War.

—— **6** ——

From where Pedersen, Carter, and Berry started, the trip to Seoul wasn't complicated, just slow. In reserve, the Fifth Regiment was above the Imjin River, about nine miles due south of the Marine-held segment of the MLR. They headed across the river at the Freedom Gate Bridge, the first span rebuilt after the Imjin's ferocious, out-of-control performance in August.

It had been a summer for the record books. Spring ice floes and snow run-off, followed by the monsoon rains that started like clockwork the last week of June in the Imjin-Han river valley made life hell. That was expected and planned for. The quantities of water that came from those sources in 1952, however, were off the charts. Special credit went to one Typhoon Karen. Churning its way north over hundreds of miles, it was a powerful category one storm as it skirted the China coast. Arcing west and crossing South Korea on the diagonal, Karen dropped down to a tropical storm. But 60-mile-an-hour wind-driven rain was far more than the guys dug in along the 38th Parallel bargained for, or that the river could handle. It rose 30 feet in 12 hours, surging forward with such might that it damaged or ripped away every bridge along its course in South Korea. Of the 11 spans, five washed out.

South of Freedom Gate, Pedersen and his cohorts passed the town of Munsan-ni, where the U.N. representatives to the peace talks were staying. From there, they picked up Highway Number One, the main link in the Western Sector between the North Korean border and Seoul. The name sounded grander than the road which, like virtually all roads on the peninsula was either dirt or hard-pack dirt and gravel. But unlike many others that flooded and turned to muck in the rainy season, Highway Number One, though unpaved, was a maintained, all-weather road. The only paved road in South Korea at that time was to the west, a five-mile stretch that ran from the outskirts of Seoul toward Inchon, and that wasn't on their itinerary.

Once they had crossed the river, the country took on a different look. Between the Imjin and the front line, the territory had been bombed, burned, and cleared of any local inhabitants, even those tenacious enough to have held fast when the North Koreans first swept through. All that remained were military personnel and the occasional interlopers, be they spies or farmers. South it was different, the country still war torn but beginning to struggle back. Driving along, the trio passed peasant villages set in from the road, some intact, others badly damaged. Plumes of smoke rose from the side chimneys of dwellings, venting wood fires burning in pits beneath the houses to keep them warm. In striking contrast to what war had done to the country's infrastructure, the land itself was beautiful, bursting with fall colors, the roads between hamlets lined with elegant poplars.

The country roads—including the one the guys were traveling—were not made for speed. They were maybe 18 feet wide, and on a clear stretch you could probably do 30 miles an hour, maybe a little more. When motor vehicles met pedestrians—the papasans with loaded A-frames strapped to their bodies, and mamasans carrying large bundles on their heads—it meant braking to a crawl to keep from covering everyone in clouds of yellow dust. Pedersen drove to Seoul periodically when the regiment was in reserve, sometimes taking a truck so members of the platoon could come along for a few hours' break.

He knew what the city looked like, but anyone seeing it for the first time had to find it jarring.

What Pedersen and his two companions saw as they drove through Seoul that morning was, as many remembered it, an awful mess. Six months after the battle that had again restored the capital to the South Koreans, things were little changed from the immediate aftermath. Buildings remained severely damaged, many gutted and burned, and debris was still piled in side streets and along main thoroughfares. Some estimates put the number of ruined structures at well over 200,000. United Nations troops occupied the city, and by 1952, Seoul was again filling with people, many homeless coming in droves from rural areas. The population, swelling to some two and a half million, was nearly a million more than before the South was invaded.

Most inhabitants still crowded into neighborhoods north of the Han River, as they had throughout Seoul's long history. The site of major settlements for 2,000 years, Seoul became the seat of the Chosun Dynasty in 1392. For centuries, well before Western countries reached similar achievements, it flourished as a center of the fine arts, education, and government. Monuments to its history—among them, massive city gates and great temples from the late 14th century—survived occupations and then war, standing amidst rubble with few scars.

The three drove into the capital from the northwest, then headed east on a road that cut across the northern part of the city. Ahead of them, in the neighborhood of Sinseol-dong, was the old Seoul racetrack. It was in a less congested part of the city, according to a U.S. Army map of the late 1940s. North of the track, a railroad connected it to the central city; to the south was a polluted little stream, Cheonggyecheon, with shacks edging its banks. Woodland areas dotted the surroundings here and there, and rice paddies flourished in corners of the track grounds, across the racecourse from the grandstand and the crowds. A few commercial buildings were nearby including, appropriately, a slaughterhouse and a fertilizer factory.

Horseracing was a popular weekend attraction, one that appealed to the Japanese, as well, and they had allowed it to flourish during their years of occupation. With the outbreak of the Korean War, however, it came to an abrupt halt, appropriately perhaps with one last hoorah: on the Sunday the North Koreans invaded, the crowd did not disperse until every race on the card was run. Thereafter, like the rest of the city, the racetrack and surroundings were destroyed. Yet, supporting the truth of war making strange bedfellows, within a year it underwent an intriguing resurrection.

The Racetrack had kept its name and was at the same location as before. Only instead of a place where someone could place a bet on the favorite, or maybe a long shot, now it was an airstrip and, at that, one of the busiest flight hubs in the Far East. It was a single runway, incoming and outgoing planes taking their turn, and it buzzed all day long. Big planes used Kimpo, South Korea's main airfield, about 35 miles west of Seoul. The Racetrack was short-hop central.

The grounds had been converted into an airfield for the U.S. Eighth Army Flight Detachment, and from there the unit's 20-plus pilots flew military personnel, statesmen, dignitaries, and entertainers around the combat theater. Even President-Elect Dwight D. Eisenhower, on his surprise trip to South Korea in early December 1952, used The Racetrack for trips to visit frontline units. The list of entertainers read like Saturday night at The Brown Derby in Los Angeles, California, or The Stork Club in New York City—from Marilyn Monroe, Debbie Reynolds, and Jane Russell, to Bob Hope, Donald O'Connor, Mickey Rooney, and on and on. It was a continuous parade, sent by the USO to do, in all, over 5,000 troop shows, with most everyone needing to be flown to where they were going to perform.

Pilots frequently flew three and four flights a day, taking passengers or correspondence to various units and bringing others back to Seoul. From morning to night, the dirt and dust barely settled on the airstrip. And amidst all the hubbub, incongruously perhaps, in the infield of the old track Korean horsemen tended crops, while around the periphery, their horses hung out in what remained of the stalls.

Pedersen had planned to head for The Racetrack. There was no need to look around Seoul. He knew what had become of the old track, that it had a new life, but he also understood the tenacity of horsemen. His gut told him some would still be there, hanging around the fringes, taking care of their stock just as they had done before. Even if they weren't sure what the future held, where would they go? Life on the racetrack is all about hope—for another day, another horse. With the war dragging on, however, Pedersen also figured that despite their hope for the future, someone would have something for sale.

What he had in mind is anyone's guess, but whether mare or gelding, it certainly had to be small enough to ride in the trailer they brought. If he knew anything about Korean racing, he knew that was what he would find. For his purposes, a small animal was also practical—easier to handle, to house, and to transport, plus just simply less for an enemy target. Parking the rig, Pedersen and the other two walked from stall to stall, sizing up one prospect and the next, then moving on. Until he saw Reckless.

———— **7** ————

She came to the Marines with a back-story, though whether true or apocryphal is open to debate. Reckless' first biographer, Andrew Geer, acknowledged that the language barrier and the lack of skilled interpreters made pursuing the story difficult. As it went, she was owned by a Korean man who had grown up on the racetrack before World War II. His name, Kim Huk Moon, was fictitious and nothing could be verified by the Korean Racing Authority. What was his real name? Did he exist at all? Or was the story that led to Reckless the quintessential racing story of a youngster who falls in love with the racetrack? Indeed, it may have been the legend of Reckless, before that very real day when she met the U.S. Marines.

Whatever her origin, the story endured with her. The youngster, from a poor Korean family in Seoul, passed the track and was drawn to the fence and the beautiful horses beyond. Little by little, he worked his way inside to do odd jobs, helping out whenever he had the chance. He showed that he had a way with horses and was given responsibilities. Happily, he walked horses after their workout to cool them down, groomed them, mucked stalls, and took care of the riding equipment.

One day someone hoisted him up on a horse. Feet in the irons, hands on the reins, he picked up a trot, riding big loops near the barn. He showed his ability and was given more mounts. He won races, but injuries intervened and he turned to training. He was given a good horse and together they won race after race.

The lore of the racetrack has many variations, the story many endings. In Reckless' case, the champion horse had a foal at the end of her long racing career. A few days later, she was dead of a raging infection. Heartbroken, the Korean trainer named the foal after her mother, Flame of the Morning. For short, he called her Flame. In light workouts, she showed speed and her trainer had visions of her future winning races. But on the backstretch that fateful Sunday when the North Koreans invaded, he made an immediate decision to get Flame off the track and his family to safety.

Harnessed to a cart, the young filly, less than two years old at that point, helped her owner's family flee south to Pusan. There she remained until the war shifted back north and consolidated along the border, at which point the Korean brought her back to the track. Flame was the product of his successful past and his hopes for the future, and he didn't want to let her go. Then his sister had an accident, leaving her injured and needing help, and his priorities changed.

Pedersen looked at Flame and made his decision. Seasoned horsemen have an instinct for good horseflesh when they see it. For him, this time it was a filly, small in stature but with a build that, he believed, could carry considerable weight. He made an offer: $250.00 in American money. It was his own money, as he had planned it to be. Getting verbal approval to obtain a horse was enough in itself. Convincing the military to pay was a complication he didn't need.

When members of the military are stationed in foreign countries, they get pocket-sized language booklets courtesy of the U.S. government. Pedersen would have had one, and he had been in Korea long enough to have mastered a few simple phrases. Or perhaps Flame's trainer or one of the other horsemen there knew a little English. Or maybe it was like the old saying, "Money talks," and sign language coupled with Yankee greenbacks carried the day. In whatever way the parties made themselves known, a deal was struck. Pedersen had a horse for his men, and the Korean trainer, according to the story, could buy an artificial leg for his sister, to replace the one she lost to a land mine explosion.

Who knows if it crossed Pedersen's mind at the time, but Flame's prior experiences, at the very least exposure to the noise and activity of the airstrip, were sound training for what lay ahead. Wherever she had been, whatever else she had been asked to do, it was clear to him that she had been well cared for and treated with kindness. She was steady, unflinching, and willing to accept an outstretched hand. It was an upbringing that allowed her to move smoothly into her next life.

That she loaded into the odd little trailer, the very antithesis of a horse van, said something about her willingness to trust. The upright wooden slats they secured built up the sides a little, but her head was clear and she had a full view of the passing scene. Her only restraint was a single tie-down, using a length of rope and running it loosely from the throatlatch ring on her halter to the front edge of the trailer. With that, three Marines and a horse rolled away from The Racetrack and headed back to camp.

They drove even slower on the way back, given their concern for the passenger in tow. Up front, one or the other not driving was always turned around, watching their horse. Pedestrians along the road stopped to watch, too. The guys marveled at her balance as she rode, head up, catching the breeze. It was late afternoon when they reached camp. Approaching the gate Flame—about to be Reckless—gave the guard a direct look, then shifted her gaze to what lay ahead.

It would be a good fit, Joe Latham and Reckless. Latham had grown up in the South, working on an aunt and uncle's farm, and knew horses well. The main thing he always believed was to handle them with care. "If you're good to them, you can make them do most anything," he said. At 35, he was also one of the older guys in the platoon, like Pedersen with a number of years in the Marine Corps already under his belt. Enlisting in 1938, he remained stateside, at Camp Lejeune in North Carolina and the Naval Air Station in Florida, until he was sent to the South Pacific during World War II. When the Korean War flared up, he was back in. As the Recoilless Rifle Platoon's Gunnery Sergeant, Latham was Pedersen's right hand man, the one who kept the company functioning day-to-day. Reckless was placed in his capable hands to begin what the guys got a kick out of calling her Hoof Camp.

Her entourage followed behind as Gunny Latham led her to an open area near the motor pool, behind the sleeping tents and the mess hall. She walked willingly on a light lead rope, staying even with Latham.

He had loosely plotted out the area where he wanted her paddock to be, throwing down stakes and some coils of barbed wire at intervals around the perimeter.

No one needed to be asked to help, or given direction. The guys simply fell in, driving the stakes into the ground and stringing the wire, creating a safe place for her to stay. It wasn't big, but it was enough space for her to move about and settle in. They filled a bucket with water and found another for feed, but that was as much as they could do in the failing light.

Dinner that night came straight from the mess hall: one loaf of bread and a hefty serving of raw oatmeal. A few of the guys hung around thinking maybe they should keep her company, but Reckless didn't seem to notice. Only her fluttering eyelids were visible above the rim of the bucket as she shoved her head down to slurp up every bit of food. No problem with her appetite, someone said. She slammed the bucket with her nose a couple of times for good measure, then wandered off, head down, nosing the ground. When she found the right spot, she buckled her legs and folded herself into a mound of red fur, comfortable enough in this new place to put sleep ahead of anything else. Convinced that she was okay, the guys went off to get some chow for themselves.

Chapter Two

THE NEW RECRUIT

———— 1 ————

U The newest recruit made the trip in her own trailer, just as she had done from Seoul the week before. It was a curious sight in the midst of the trucks and tanks, a first look for plenty of guys who had missed Reckless' arrival or first days around the compound. There hadn't been any big announcement. She had arrived like any other new member of the platoon, was billeted, and started to learn the ropes. Then, within days, they were on the move again.

Trucks lumbered back and forth, taking three days to move two of the Fifth Regiment's three battalions to the front. In all, a couple thousand men plus their belongings and supplies rode the few miles north, packed in the slow, noisy motor-column. The third battalion stayed in reserve camp; the regiment waiting to be relieved maintained battle readiness until the switch was complete. On October 12, 1952, the Fifth Regiment's first and second battalions were back on line for another two months.

The destination now was the open lands east of the village of Changdan, the designated forward camp for the Fifth Regiment. Like virtually every mark of South Korean life above the Imjin River, the town had been destroyed during the war, its inhabitants killed or run off. During the Japanese occupation, Changdan had catered to the upper classes, which came to the area for the game hunting. Eerily, by 1952 one of the few vestiges of its former life was a burnt-out bank vault standing in a charred field. Northeast of town the important land markers were Hill 229 and in front of that, Hill 124, otherwise known as Hedy. In September, the enemy's attempt to grab Hedy had been roundly rebuffed by U.N. forces, but the threat of enemy action along the MLR hung in the air every day.

Almost three-quarters of the peninsula was mountainous, more rugged in the north than in the south; in the south, more rugged in the east than in the west. The Taebaek Mountains stretched like a north-south spine along the eastern part of the country, with the foothills dropping off sharply toward the Sea of Japan in the east, and rolling off more gently in the west. The terrain in the Western Sector was often likened to the inland coastal area around Camp Pendleton. Not the weather, which was colder and wetter than California, but the lower hills covered in scrub pines and other shrubs, and the broad valleys, were similar. New to the eye were the rice paddies. In good times, each would have been neatly edged with dirt berms or dikes to hold in water that flooded the valley floor. Now they were wrecked, smelly, and soggy.

At the front, the Marines were no more than half a mile from the U.N.'s MLR and the south edge of No Man's Land. When the enemy felt like harassing them, they sent shells past the usual targets to land in the midst of camp, the *wissshhh* of incoming fire a hair-raising and all too regular occurrence. Keeping Reckless safe, while an obvious need, was going to be a challenge. When the Fifth Regiment went back on line, they had known their new recruit less than two weeks, days that had been spent in the relative comfort and security of reserve camp. How she would react to the sights and sounds on the front line, no one knew. Here everyone was on heightened alert—for their own safety, for their buddies, and now, as much as they could, for Reckless. It meant keeping her penned up, as far back in camp as they could manage. The safest spot was near Regimental Headquarters, where they staked out a generous-sized paddock, then built her a bunker.

Life up front was a lot rougher than in reserve. Hot showers were out; cold water was in; food service was simplified, often coming down to heated C-rations, the military's prepackaged, non-spoiling meal packs, delivered by truck. As much as possible, tents and bunkers were set on the reverse side of hills, for the added protection of facing away from the enemy. Tents were pitched on inclines for better drainage; bunkers were dug into hillsides. Unlike reserve camp, this forward position was not fenced in. Land mines were all over South Korea, set liberally in early combat by both sides and left for others to defuse or, unsuspectingly, to step on and detonate. The camp was clear, but beyond it everyone watched where they stepped. "You could run up on mines anywhere," said Guy Wagoner. "There was always that danger. You never knew exactly where they were."

2

Reactions to Reckless were enthusiastic, though divided. Ranchers and farm boys thought the idea made perfect sense. To them, the real question was, why wouldn't they have a horse? The city types, well, they were intrigued, but also perplexed. Still, no matter what their background, the initial meeting was pretty much the same: stopping to digest the fact of what was in front of them, right there in camp, followed by assorted epithets peppered around the words, "Will ya look at that? There's a horse."

"Oh, sure, that was my first thought. What are you doing with a horse up here?" said Corporal Joe Gordon, remembering the first time he got a look at Reckless. "I was sure she was going to get spooked with all that incoming hitting our line."

Gordon was from Oahu, Hawaii, and he arrived at forward camp in November 1952. A few weeks earlier and he probably would have been pitching the game against the Tankers when Reckless showed up. He had a really strong arm and before his time in Korea was up it won him an award, the First Marine Division Zippo lighter in softball. He and several friends enlisted together, all anxious to get to Korea. For Gordon, there was some unfinished business to clear up. "I was living in Hawaii when they hit Pearl Harbor. My dad was in the Navy, so it was a tough time for me and my family," he explained. Getting to Korea and into the fight was something he felt he needed to do. At 17, his mother said no to him enlisting, but his stepfather signed him in and he headed for Camp Pendleton. As soon as he turned 18, he volunteered for the war.

Reckless was like a bit of home for Gordon. His family had a small farm out in the valley beyond Honolulu, and he grew up around horses. "I loved them from the time I was a little kid," he said. "There were a lot of them in Hawaii. Where we were, almost everyone had horses." In short order, he was taking care of the Marine's new recruit. No one asked him to help, he just did it. Watching out for her came naturally. "I bonded with that horse. She was a part of me," he said simply.

It was extraordinary how many lives Reckless affected from the very beginning, and how brightly she is remembered. "My gosh, we were proud of that little horse," said Corporal Doug Christopherson, another of the guys who knew her early on. "A horse on the front line? Why, we couldn't believe it." An Oregon farm kid, he also grew up around horses, eight of which his family used to work their land. "I'd go out to Reckless' paddock and hold her and hug her, and give her a smooch. Oh, sure, some of the other guys thought I was crazy, but she brought a little bit of home to me, too," he laughed.

Christopherson, Gordon, thousands of others—what drew these

guys to the war? The vast majority still teenagers, many enlisted right after high school graduation and turned 18 just before they arrived in Korea. They were youngsters at the close of World War II, yet old enough to be impressionable, to appreciate the excitement and drama of homecomings. They looked up to fathers and other family members, friends and neighbors returning proudly, dressed in their uniforms, showing their medals. They soaked up war movies like *Sands of Iwo Jima*, *The Story of G.I. Joe*, *Guadalcanal Diary*, *Halls of Montezuma*, and *Battleground*, played war games, and fed their boyhood memories of a previous war. And in just a few years, the Korean War gave them all their turn—the kids, and the vets who were called back to command them.

——— 3 ———

The First Marine Division, the only division in Korea, was holding down the Western Sector, a shift from their eastern position that had taken place six months prior, in March 1952. Swapping positions with the ROK troops consumed two weeks and made the Fifth Regiment's move from reserve camp to the front seem like a walk in the park. The Marines' new assignment was a hefty order, and commanders were well aware of what had been thrust upon them. They would defend an area far greater than anything normally assigned to a division. In terms of casualties, it would prove very costly.

The division's three infantry regiments were now in charge of the Jamestown Line, the 35-mile expanse of the MLR that ran from the Kimpo Peninsula, jutting into the Yellow Sea on the west, to the Samichon River on the east. Neighbors to the west were the Kimpo Provisional Regiment, an amalgam of Korean Marines with support from U.S. and other U.N. forces. To the east was the Commonwealth Division, with units from Great Britain, Canada, Australia, New Zealand, and India. Beyond them were the ROK troops, then in the far Eastern Sector was the U.S. Eighth Army. The ongoing worry to the Marines and their allies to the west was that if the Chinese breached the line on its western flank, it would open the way to Seoul through the historic north-south Uijonbu Corridor.

Midway along the Marine line was the Fifth Regiment, positioned slightly east of the north-south Peace Corridor and due south of the Peace Circle that ringed Panmunjom. The neutral areas had been set up to guarantee the safe passage of participants in the Peace Talks—representatives from North Korea, who were living in Kaesong, to the west of Panmunjom, and U.N. representatives, who were staying in Munsan-ni, headquarters of the U.N. Command, on the south side of the Freedom Gate Bridge. The talks got underway in July 1951, and stumbled along in a mostly off-again, on-again fashion, halted by the enemy for the smallest provocation. A single shell falling within any part of the safe zones would have been reason enough, and explained why such tight restrictions were in place, though obviously annoying to the opposing forces. By late October 1952 the Peace Talks were stalled again, as it would turn out, for another six months.

The parties first sat around the table in Kaesong, but in short order moved their discussions east to the scruffy village of Panmunjom. The Peace Circle that was superimposed was roughly a mile and a quarter in diameter, from east of Kaesong to the outskirts of the tiny hamlet of Kamon-dong. In the center, at Panmunjom, a huge searchlight aimed its beam straight into the night sky, a beacon to pilots to keep outside of the circle's perimeter. A second, shorter Peace Corridor connected Kaesong to the circle. Both corridors were buffered along their entire lengths by quarter-mile, no-fire strips on each side. The restrictions were simple. There could be no arms fire of any kind into or over any part of the No Fire Zone, circle and corridors.

The ground configuration and the difficulties it imposed on combat were a continuing aggravation to the Fifth Regiment. Both sides looked for ways to fire on the other's positions near the neutral zones, the trick being to do it in a way that kept the opposition from returning fire and risking shells landing in any part of the off-limits area. By turn, combatants took the upper hand, and on the day after the Fifth Marines came back on line, it was the Communist Chinese who were firing on a company that was manning a forward outpost. The enemy's shield was the low-lying buildings of Kamon-dong, which were being used as a supply depot. The outpost the enemy was targeting was southeast of them, and far enough away from the Peace Corridor that their attack would not cause any breach in diplomatic relations.

The Marines were having no such luck. If they returned fire, they risked shells landing within the neutral zone; the space between Kamon-dong and the eastern edge of the circle was that close. But Pedersen and First Battalion Commander Alexander Gentlemen, shifted the advantage by moving a recoilless rifle into a position where it could be fired but not fired upon. The spot was the intersection of the north-south Peace Corridor and the Circle—an inside elbow of sorts—where the rifle could be positioned within a couple of steps to neutral territory. From there, with the accuracy of the recoilless rifle, gunners began demolishing Kamon-dong, targeting the buildings one by one, from the eastern most edge of the village inward. In short order, the structures crumbled and the few inhabitants fled.

Again, there was difficulty in getting ammunition to the gun site. Driving a truckload of shells up the Peace Corridor would have been the simplest solution. Except it was a violation of neutrality and, thus, not allowed. Again, it meant the guys picked up the slack. Ammunition was trucked to the forward outpost, and from there lugged on foot the last half mile to the gun site. Looking ahead, however, Pedersen was reassured. Reckless wasn't ready to show her stuff yet, but buying her looked like it was a smart move.

—— **4** ——

The war was marching in place. Some people called it static, others a stalemate. Basically, as the peace talks crawled along, the job of the U.N. forces was to hold the main line while, at the same time, the enemy tried to eke out more territory. Small, localized actions, largely concerned with maintaining or retaking key combat outposts, broke out along the line. The enemy encroached, U.N. forces checked them; U.N. forces took back the territory, the enemy retreated. Over and over, it dragged on. Aggressive patrols gathered information, returned fire, and determined where to direct further combat action.

By the end of October 1952, it was cold. Sports tournaments had wrapped up, with Fifth Regiment units taking victories in division basketball, football, and track. Movies remained a constant, shown every night, just like in reserve. Snow was starting to fall, and the supply depots were issuing cold-weather gear for the dreaded Korean winter. According to the Regiment's command diary, each man was given a parka, pile field jacket, field jacket hood, alpaca vest, wool socks, mittens, pile field cap, wool muffler, flannel shirt, wool field trousers, wool undershirt, wool drawers, leather glove shells, high neck sweater, and Arctic overshoes. There were also winter sleeping bags and kerosene stoves.

Reckless, meanwhile, took care of herself, growing a coat that was heavier and more impervious to the cold than any fur parka available. Though early in the season, the look was clear: longer hair on the face, especially around the jowls and chin; a thick covering on the neck, sides and underneath; a thick all-over torso cover, including plenty on the belly to keep her warm when she laid down; and long leg hair, top to hoof. Winter growth gave Reckless a distinctively shaggy, rounded appearance.

Life with Reckless started out nice and easy. That was the Latham touch at work. With a saddle still to arrive, there was time to break her in slowly. It gave her a chance to settle down, become comfortable with her surroundings, and show who she was or might become. An enjoyment of the limelight was certainly a part of her personality, and her fellow Marines quickly obliged. She carried rank, private first class, and serial number 1-H soon after she arrived. To the guys it seemed totally appropriate. She was one of the Reckless Marines, no question about that

Platoon members who had completed their tours of duty and were heading home, never remembered anything more than the fun of having a beloved pet in camp. If they asked, they were told of future plans for Reckless, but for the present she just seemed to be hanging out. Corporal Roland Bergstrom, about to head back to Minnesota, couldn't picture her as a workhorse, not with her "spindly legs," as he called them. The horses he knew, growing up on a farm, were big, sturdy, heavy-boned types, and his opinion was that she was "just not suitable" for what the Marines had in mind. Not that it mattered, given the enthusiasm she created. "We had tons of fun with her when she was out in the fenced area," he recalled. "One of us was always going over there. We'd give her crackers and candy. It could be kind of boring, the time got long, and she was a great morale booster."

From the start, Reckless proved to be quite the good eater, which is to say there was little she didn't think was fine fare. Latham, Gordon, and others who pitched in to care for Reckless tried to moderate her diet when they could, but the stories that survive attest to a great deal of give and take. Latham's choice of her first dinner—bread and raw oatmeal along with a bucket of water—would have been a variation on a bran mash, something that horsemen will feed after a long and stressful day. Pedersen is thought to have brought some type of horse feed back the day they got Reckless, although there wouldn't have been space for much. Thereafter, Latham purchased what grain he could from local farmers, but during harsh times the guys fanned out in the hills and pulled whatever grass they could find for her to eat.

Gordon, treating her as he did his horses in Hawaii, made sure she had plenty of fruit in her diet, which she scoffed down with relish. Then there was mess hall food, and often that is what she ate. On the front line, where she was fenced in, she had to rely on what her buddies would share with her. But even in those first weeks, newcomer that she was, her "please feed me" skills were well developed. By late December, when the regiment was back in reserve camp she roamed free, and the mess hall was part of her daily rounds. The list of her likes, when she could get her way, was as varied as a good diner menu and then some, and included but was hardly limited to: scrambled eggs, bacon, shredded wheat, toast, crackers, pancakes (no syrup, please), peanut butter sandwiches, cherry pie, candy bars, and Coca Cola. On the side, she also enjoyed beer, an occasional mixed drink and even, now and then, a whiskey or two. "She'd come up to the mess and try to eat everything," Gordon laughed. "But we watched out for her as best we could. We didn't have her going wild." The couple of stomach upsets the guys remembered subsided on their own with no treatment needed. Whatever the combination between horse-appropriate grains and grass and the rest of what Reckless could get hold of, she thrived on it.

—— 5 ——

When the guys weren't calling, "Hey, Reckless," they would call her their small horse or mare. Many described her as a "pretty thing" and, given her diminutive size, some even called her a pony. Nothing more detailed seemed to be known, nor did Andrew Geer shed any light on her breeding. Through the years, some people began calling her a Mongolian horse and, indeed, still do, though without any evidence to confirm it. One explanation may be that the Mongolian horse is the best known of Asia's native breeds, and in Korea's long-ago past, the country endured a period of Mongol occupation. Reckless, however, was something different, with a unique and intriguing history specific to Korea and celebrated to the present day.

Reckless, in all probability, was a Jeju pony, the only equine breed native to her country. Given that she came from the racetrack, it puzzled the Marines how something that small could have been a racehorse or, to be exact, one who was expected to have a racing career when war was over. Judged against racing stock in the U.S. and other parts of the Western World, it made no sense. Yet, the answer was right in front of them, because the equines raced at tracks in Korea were Jeju ponies, a practice that would continue until the mid-1970s. Geer gave one clue in his lead up to Reckless' life with the Marine Corps, when he mentioned that her dam had raced for 12 years. While occasionally, a thoroughbred will have a racing career of seven or eight years, anything beyond that happens infrequently. Jeju ponies, on the other hand, have been known to still race at age 20.

In Korean, Jejus are also called Jejuma or Gwahama, meaning "short enough to go under fruit trees." Their average height at the withers—the point of the equine anatomy where the neck joins the back—is 11 to 12 hands or 44 to 48 inches (a hand equals four inches) and at that, with head ducked, they can clear some of the lowest hanging branches. They can look very pony-like, with short, stocky legs, or have more horse-like proportions, notably with longer, slimmer legs. Reckless was one of the latter.

Jejus come in the basic equine colors of chestnut, as was Reckless; gray, which whitens with age; black; and bay, or dark brown. There are also pintos, with splotchy black and white, or brown and white coats. Their ancestral homeland is Jeju Island off the southern tip of the South Korean mainland. A beautiful but rugged spot, it is known for dramatic weather swings from hot summers to snowy winters, and is regularly struck by typhoons and monsoon rains. The pony that evolved there was an extremely strong and resilient animal, prized according to earliest records by Korean kings and conquerors alike.

As early as 1073, the Korean ruler, Emperor Munjong, was gifted with the finest steeds from the herds of native Jejus. Two centuries later, when the Mongols overran the peninsula and, crossing the Korea Strait, took Jeju Island, as well, they were equally quick to appreciate the ponies they found. Over the next hundred years, during their occupation of Korea, the Mongols selectively bred their horses to the Korean ponies. However, researchers now believe it was not their native Mongolian horses that were bred, as was previously assumed. Genetic testing now shows that this archaic breed has been little altered by human-induced crossbreeding, and is today virtually unchanged from its early existence. Apparently, the Mongols appreciated their native breed for its natural attributes.

As it turns out, it was the Ferghana horse that the Mongols chose to crossbreed, an import acquired by the thousands following an earlier victory in the present-day region of Turkmenistan in Central Asia. These were the blood-sweating horses of ancient writings that appeared, quite literally, to sweat blood after a long, sustained gallop—as recorded, some 25 miles at a stretch. Researchers theorize that a parasite common to the Russian steppes burrowed subcutaneously into the horses' hides, creating skin nodules that bled under stress. Fortunately, whatever the appeal of the Ferghana's skin, it was not transmitted to the Jejus, at least not to the liking of any parasite with which the latter came in contact.

Toward the end of the 13th century, the Mongols sent 160 of their finest Ferghana horses to Jeju, along with many expert horsemen, and over the next hundred years they returned a steady supply of what they bred to the Mongolian Empire in China. When the Koreans finally expelled the Mongols, their horsemen, by then several generations assimilated into Korean life, stayed behind. Though it is unknown exactly what characteristics were prized above others, the long-sustained breeding program was worthwhile, not only to the Mongols, but as well to the Koreans. The small, hardy ponies that remained on Jeju Island were the foundation of an important and versatile fixture of Korean life, prized for hundreds of years in various roles. In the Chosun Dynasty, emperors received 300 Jejus a year at the royal court in Seoul. For the common man, owning a native pony was considered a privilege.

Breeding Jeju ponies became the sustaining industry on Jeju Island for centuries. By the 1600s, there were 20,000 Jeju ponies on the island, spread over numerous breeding farms, a ready supply exported to the mainland for farming and transportation. The ponies were also a food source on the island, at times the only meat available. Even today, some restaurants on Jeju Island serve dishes made with pony meat, an acknowledgment to the animal that sustained them, quite literally, in good times and bad.

Tough was an apt description for the Jejus—a trait that was deeply ingrained and, at times, of jaw-dropping intensity. In the remote world of Korea before the Japanese occupation, travelers had limited means of getting around the country. They could walk, be carried aloft in a chair borne by bearers, or ride a shaggy little Jeju pony. Sure-footed and strong, ponies could carry a good-sized adult 30 miles or more a day over the roughest terrain. The choice of a pony or ponies—one to ride and, if needed, a second to carry baggage—were always stallions, and came with a handler or mapoo to keep the wily creatures under control. It didn't always work, said Robert Neff, a writer for the *Korea Times* and Jeju historian, recounting the experiences of some unsuspecting Westerners who witnessed the often-raucous behavior of the little native ponies:

A British diplomat described travelers who opted to use the ponies as "invariably afforded an unfailing source of amusement and irritation..." A young American missionary recalled how "two of those poor little pack-ponies which I had been pitying all along for the terrible way their relentless mapoos overloaded them, began fighting (loads and all), and after kicking each other in the liveliest fashion for some time, squealing like little fiends, while the poor mapoos were dancing and vociferating around them trying to bring about a truce, they finally scampered off in different directions, and then and there my heart hardened and never since has pity for these animals entered it. They are, I firmly opine, as self-willed, spoiled, obstinate, quarrelsome, uncertain, tricky and tough little beasts as ever carried a load." And another visitor characterized the Jejus as "indeed the trickiest little devils for their size I have ever seen, and for viciousness and love of fighting, equine wickedness in the Realm of the Morning Calm," their behavior in sharp contrast with the ancient name for Korea.

Their notorious reputation was sufficient to bring a group of Jejus to American shores, booked as a sideshow by the elaborately titled, "Sells Brothers Enormous Roman Hippodrome Double Elevated Stage & Five

Continent Menagerie, United With S.H. Barrett's Monster World's Fair" during the show's Galveston, Texas run in November 1889. A poster from the times promoted them as "Bun Yip or Devil Horses from the Wicked Harem of Soribad, King of Corea," the fictitious ruler and odd spelling of Korea obviously of no concern to the show's promoters.

––––––– 6 –––––––

The Jeju became Korea's racehorse in the early 20th century. The sport developed, as it does in most countries, beginning with informal meets, held locally and usually with little pre-planning. Like others, Koreans used the equine stock that was on hand—in their case, the same native pony that was already working the farms and transporting heavy loads. It wasn't Western-style racing, nor was there any reason for it to be. Racing Jeju ponies was distinctively Korean, and as the sport increased in popularity during the Japanese occupation, its native character must have been a particular point of pride. Japan continued to undermine many aspects of Korean life, but racing Jeju ponies was not one of them.

Local race tracks sprang up across the peninsula and, by 1922, with the establishment of the Chosun Racing Club, the sport's first official efforts to coordinate and control racing nationally were underway. Pari-mutual betting, or betting the track's odds, was available, though always with the choice to take the bookies' odds, albeit illegally. And local tracks could operate, so long as they did so under incorporated racing clubs. In 1928, Chosun opened the Seoul Race Track at Sinseol-dong, the country's first official track.

The Seoul track was the big time, and a popular place to be on weekends when the ponies ran. Judged against the legend on a U.S. Army map of 1946, the racing oval was not much smaller than many racetracks today, although pony races were (and still are) shorter than races for larger horses. Videos from the 1960s show Korean jockeys sitting the gallop and riding with long stirrups. The style had been used much earlier in Western racing, though jockeys had since switched to "riding short," with legs jacked up high on the mount's sides and feet in short stirrups. However, given how much less animal body mass was under the Korean jockey, plus the amazing agility of a pony—not necessarily to the benefit of a rider—Korean riders knew what they were doing in keeping more of their weight back and on the saddle.

Post World War II, the Korea Racing Authority (KRA) continued the work of the Chosun organization in managing the sport. At the Seoul Race Track, it owned all the ponies. There was no prize money and track personnel—including trainers, jockeys, and grooms—were paid by the KRA. Both practices, as internal matters, in no way diminished the enthusiasm of the racegoers. Track regulars in the late 1940s included a number of noted South Koreans, among them President Syngman Rhee; Shin Ik Hee, speaker of the country's National Assembly; and another popular politician and writer, Kim Gu, otherwise known as The Ordinary Man. Above the grandstand and the betting parlor, they watched the action from the vantage of the third floor VIP lounge. The KRA acknowledged their support with races named in their honor.

There was no formal means of identification for the Jeju ponies racing in those years, no photographs, no tattoos, certainly nothing like the current practice of micro-chipping the Jejus that race. Nevertheless, if Reckless was a part of the racing community, stabled at what was left of the Seoul Race Track, even as it functioned as a U.S. Army airstrip, it is virtually certain she was a Jeju pony. Whether she had been on the racetrack before the war, as Geer contended, or came to that point when she joined the Marines from a different set of circumstances, is a matter of conjecture, the original story left wanting in some respects. However, in the company of racetrackers that day in October 1952, racing would certainly be in her cards. Whatever else is true, the Marines bought a Jeju pony and had her life taken a different direction, she would most surely have been a racehorse.

At Sinseol-dong, the name locals often gave to the Seoul Race Track, the events of June 25, 1950, unfolded piece by piece, reluctantly closing an era. Racing would never come back to the country's premier track. North Korean troops invaded the South in the pre-dawn hours, breaching the 38th Parallel at points across the breadth of the country. Yet, even in the late morning, as the grandstand filled and rumors of the invasion began to spread, the news did not seem to unsettle the crowd. Cross-border skirmishes were old news, and that day Shin Ik Hee was being honored with one of the biggest races of the year.

It was a pleasant summer day with temperatures in the 70s. Racing got underway at 11:00 a.m., the first three races being run without incident. But before the fourth race, an unidentified plane came into view and circled overhead, dropping hundreds of leaflets onto the spectators and field. The message to South Koreans: their "liberation" was underway. Soon, military jeeps arrived at the track and through loud speakers, directed all soldiers on leave to return immediately to their units.

Yet, racing fans stayed on, perhaps refusing to accept the reality of what was long expected. The seventh race, for Shin Ik Hee, went off as scheduled, as did the remaining five races. The events of the past few hours, however, confirmed the worst. South Korea had been invaded. At 5:00 p.m., after the last race, all young men still on the track—mostly trainers, jockeys, and grooms—were told to report to the racing office for induction into the military.

And Reckless, if she was at the track that day, what happened to her? She had not raced yet but, according to Geer, she was in training and that would have put her on the backside of the track, stabled with the other horses. From there her original story becomes complicated when her trainer, so it was said, took her south, along with his family, to safety in Pusan. Did this young pony, hitched to a cart, really travel nearly 250 miles south, on roads clogged with hordes of fleeing refugees, amidst the North Korean troops advancing down the peninsula and ROK troops retreating? What Geer didn't acknowledge is the fact that Reckless would have been owned by the KRA and not her trainer, though his desire to protect her would have been understandable. Even if she wasn't his, did he take her off the track anyway? Or is Reckless' story before she met her Marines something simpler and more direct?

Sinseol-dong closed that Sunday and racing was suspended, though for how long no one knew at the time. Three days later, when Seoul was captured, the racetrack was turned into a supply depot by the North Koreans. In the third week of September, after the Inchon invasion, U.N. forces liberated the capital. It was a hard-fought victory; Seoul was in ruins. Nevertheless, with the success of Inchon, South Korea and its allies were encouraged to believe that the war would soon be over. The KRA, joining in the optimism, began plans to restart racing, perhaps as early as late October.

The reality of what had happened at the racetrack upset those prospects. Racing officials had not taken into consideration how desperate the battle for Seoul had been. Fighting went door to door, street to street. The supply depot was a prime target for U.N. bombing. Unprepared for what they would find, when racing officials saw the track, they were appalled. They reported total devastation: the buildings destroyed, the safe looted, and the horses gone. It was presumed the horses were either taken north after the initial invasion, or killed at the time or when the U.N. forces, retaking the city, bombed the depot.

Still, hope lingered. The KRA made arrangements for a new group of Jeju ponies to be shipped up from the South. Almost as quickly,

Communist China entered the war, standing by its declaration to come to the defense of North Korea if U.N. forces pushed north. With that, chances for a quick end to the war were dashed, and it went on for another 33 months.

Racing never came back to Sinseol-dong, though the core of the old track's racing community gravitated back to the place they knew. It would have been their comfort zone. They settled around the periphery for the rest of the war, caring for ponies, probably some of that new crop still waiting to run. Geer contended that when the fighting morphed into trench warfare along the 38th Parallel, Reckless' trainer brought her back from Pusan. Or did her story really start in the fall of 1950, when she came from Jeju Island, part of the KRA's hope for racing's comeback?

No ponies raced again until after the war ended, and whether all of that first new crop made it to the track or were siphoned off to do other work is unknown. When racing restarted in May 1954, it was at a new track, Ttukseom, across town from Sinseol-dong. Construction had been started by the KRA during the war. Ponies still raced, all owned by the track—until the late 1970s, when the KRA adopted Western-style racing and switched to running Thoroughbreds.

By then, the Jejus' numbers were in decline. In the post war years, South Korea evolved from its rural, agrarian past to a booming, industrialized country. The large numbers of Jejus needed for farming dwindled and by the 1980s, there were as few as 2,500 ponies in country. Their value had been marginalized, and they were shipped to Japan for meat and elsewhere for pet food. Fortunately, the government stepped in. The Jeju Pony was designated National Monument 347, and in 1990 a racetrack was opened on Jeju Island, exclusively for pony racing.

Today, the Jejus run every Friday and Saturday throughout the year, their races simulcast to the KRA's two other tracks—the new Seoul Race Park, in the suburb of Gwancheon, which replaced Ttukseon in 1989, and a track in Busan. On Jeju, the horse industry flourishes, with farms breeding thoroughbreds as well as the native pony. But it is the Jeju ponies alone that are celebrated in a festival each fall, a reminder of their place in the history and economy of the country. Among them, it should be noted, a young mare did her part for South Korea in that country's last war.

—— 7 ——

Reckless, you might say, was a cool customer. She was comfortable around people, and unflappable beyond expectations. Wherever she had been, she had been well treated. At The Racetrack, when it had been converted to Seoul's busy wartime airstrip, she was within earshot of planes and helicopters taking off and landing from dawn to dusk. She had undoubtedly had visitors who wondered what horses were doing at an airfield. All of it, from affection to commotion, had paid dividends. The front line, so far as Reckless' new handlers could tell in the first couple of months she was with them, wasn't causing her any concern.

At some point, so Pedersen figured, the future racehorse had been broken to saddle. It was one thing he or Latham wouldn't have to do when the saddle arrived. The type he had in mind was unlike anything she had been used to on the track, but as long as she had carried weight on her back, which he guessed she had, it was a step in the right direction. Pedersen hadn't asked his wife's help until Reckless was actually on base. Then he wrote Katherine, back in San Diego, California, telling her what he had purchased, and that he needed a packsaddle. A veterinarian friend turned up a used one, and Katherine's father crated and shipped it out. Pedersen's wife, always behind her husband's love of horses, felt if this one could help his men, she was all for his plan.

The saddle took ten weeks to arrive, a lull that gave Latham time to teach Reckless some basics of frontline survival. Her instincts were sharp and she picked things up quickly. The terrain was rough around the Fifth Regiment's forward position, and surefooted as horses are, Latham was taking no chances. She needed to step over the communications wires that were laid around camp and the forward hills, and not snag them with her hooves. Latham and Pedersen both walked her around, showing her what they wanted. A photograph of her working with Latham shows her looking at the ground intently, as if absorbing her lesson well.

More impressive was her ability to get out of harm's way. If she and Latham couldn't get themselves to cover when enemy shells started exploding in camp, they would both hit the ground. "I taught her that when I put my hand on her hoof, she should fall down," he said, describing how he would touch her and crouch down himself. Amazingly, she would copy him, buckling her legs and folding into a heap beside him. But it was her quick-wittedness when she was in her paddock and shells came raining down that had the Marines shaking their heads in wonder.

"One time we started getting incoming fire," remembered Sergeant Pete Kitral, from Lyle, Illinois, one of the squad leaders in the Recoilless Rifle Platoon. "She was in her paddock and shells were landing all over." Kitral dashed out to look for Reckless, praying he could get to her before she got hit.

"I couldn't see her anywhere," he recalled. "I figured for sure she was dead." Just then, he saw a nose—her nose—poking, ever so slightly, out of the entrance to her bunker. "She was already in there," Kitral marveled. "She knew enough to get herself inside that bunker."

Latham, it turned out, had again shown her what he wanted, several times when shells hit, hollering "incoming, incoming" and making a mad dash for her bunker—with Reckless right on his heels. "She was no dummy," he chuckled. "When that incoming started, we would all scramble into our bunkers, and she would head for hers." He admitted, though, that times when she was outside her paddock, hanging out with the guys as they loved having her do, when the shelling began she would head for the most convenient bunker—piling right in behind her buddies.

With the cold weather, combat settled into the repetitive pattern of patrols, shelling, ambushes, and raids. Nothing for the time being suggested enemy troop build-ups and looming battles, but there was still plenty of action to keep nerves edgy—like the day Reckless ran away.

What made her do it, no one was sure, but it sent a chill through camp. Latham tried to keep it as quiet as possible, but those who knew were scared. She had wandered off, just where was anyone's guess, but as close as they were to the front line, the consequences could be dire. Land mines were as much a worry as ever. All along the front line, troops kept defusing them, but it was an endless effort. If Reckless stepped on one, that would be the finish of her. Winding up in North Korea would be, too.

Ponies from the North that made it to the South were the lucky ones. Some of them wandered off like Reckless had done, others were stampeded across No Man's Land in the black of night, tripping wires and setting off flares, causing an immediate "highest alert" and Marines on guard to fire their weapons. But the guys knew if she went the other way and reached enemy territory, she wouldn't get back.

"We couldn't pay attention to her all the time," said Kitral, sounding frustrated at the memory. "Look, we were at war. We were trying to stay alive ourselves." A few of the guys, Kitral among them, were yet to be convinced that having Reckless around, even though the plan sounded good, was a really wise move. Like some of them said, as a mascot and morale booster, sure. But Kitral, for one, was concerned that she could jeopardize the men's safety. This was such a time.

The Marines fanned out, going beyond base as far as they dared.

"No one had any idea which direction she'd gone. Everybody searched, as much as we were allowed without being in too much danger ourselves," remembered Doug Christopherson. Latham knew the North Koreans were aware of Reckless and would like to grab her. "I thought they were going to get her that day," he admitted, "but we got her back in time. They'd have eaten that horse. Oh, yeah, they were trying to get hold of her."

She got loose, Latham found out later, because "somebody was playing around with her out at that little corral I had for her. She didn't really know that many of the guys yet, and if she didn't take a liking to you right off, she'd kick at you. Whoever was there didn't pick up on that quick enough and she broke out and ran off." Latham was furious. He never said who did it, but he knew.

She was gone about a day, and then they got a lead. When they spotted her, she took one look at Latham and came right to him. She seemed happy to be back, Christopherson thought. "Was she just feeling her oats, curious to see if there was something over that next hill? Then maybe what she saw, she didn't like?" he wondered. Among those who knew what had happened, the sigh of relief was almost palpable. It also reminded everyone of how new she still was to her surroundings.

Reckless' saddle arrived in December, close to the holidays as the guys remembered it. Pedersen's wife had opted for a used saddle, which was practical considering the battering it was going to take. The most popular make around would have been a Phillips, the type of packsaddle used for many years by the U.S. Cavalry. It was quite the invention, capable of supporting cargo yet leaving the horse comfortable and able to move freely at all gaits. Back pads were held in place by an assortment of straps buckling across the chest and rump, and under the belly. What she thought of it all, they would find out. It was a good bet that

Reckless had never had such a contraption on her back.

If there was any worry, it turned out to be groundless. The heavier, less flexible saddle was settled on Reckless' back without incident. Latham was always gentle and reassuring in working with her, and she had come to trust him. But they were going to be adding a great deal more weight —bulky, awkward, heavy shells—all dead weight that she would have to deal with. Historically, a Jeju often carried its cargo on an A-frame secured to the back, the weight centered over the horse's midsection with the heaviest items close to its body. The shells were longer, and she would be climbing uphill with them. It would be a challenge. On top of the saddle, they added a pannier, another system of straps, sometimes with side bags, to support the load evenly. Latham made a mental note to keep the weight as moderate as possible when he could. He knew when called upon, this tough little pony could do more.

Just before Christmas, they put the whole moving process in reverse. Trucks hauled the Fifth Regiment from the front line back to reserve camp, this time over snow covered, icy roads. Private First Class Reckless rode in her trailer, just one of the guys, although not jammed into one of the big trucks like a lot of her buddies. Latham had sharpened her trailering skills, working with her so that jumping in and out of that box on two wheels was something she did when asked. Horsemen all have their stories about the ones that are not nearly so accommodating. At the front, however, when the recoilless rifle guys had to move out, she had to load without hesitation.

Some guys thought there might have been a paddock and shed for her, either newly built or the old holdover, but everyone agreed, Reckless was never in it. This time back in reserve, the whole camp was her domain. The fence around the perimeter and the guard at the gate kept her inside, the biggest concern. Joe Gordon remembered her keeping warm behind the big hot water tanks outside the mess hall, and other guys made room for her at night when she decided to sleep in one of their tents. Whether or not she saw the USO show that month, or any of the nightly movies, is not known. It is a sure bet, though, that Reckless enjoyed her very own Christmas dinner with all the trimmings.

At the end of January 1953 the Fifth Regiment packed up and headed back to the front line. Combat activity was still down, but constant like a muffled roar. Some were uneasy that the relative quiet couldn't last. Whatever the threat level, the rest of Reckless' training would be in real time. The horse the Marines loved would soon show them if she was the horse they needed.

Chapter Three

ON THE LINE

—— 1 ——

U If it wasn't that everyone got so damned tired, dragging themselves up those hills, they would have laughed at how quickly Reckless showed them up. She was that fast. Guys would be crawling up a hill, hauling their equipment, and up she would come. Carrying at least four shells strapped to her packsaddle, she would move past her buddies, wait on the ridge while someone unloaded the ammunition, and be half way back down before the other guys made it all the way up.

Hills and more hills or, as the men would describe it, climb to the top of one hill and another was staring you in the face. Looking over No Man's Land from the U.N. side, that was the view—hills mounded one behind the other, going back like so many Slinky toys into the far distance, interrupted at intervals by valleys filled with ruined rice paddies.

It was a landscape for a mountain goat—and, it soon became apparent, for a Jeju pony, as well, and Reckless' physical attributes showed why. Low to the ground, with a short turning radius and strong frame, she combined all that with the sure footedness evolved from hundreds of years roaming the foothills of Halla-san, the highest mountain in South Korea, located on Jeju Island. Whatever could have been said of her future as a racehorse, the characteristics were tailor-made for her new life at the front line.

As soon as the saddle arrived, Latham stepped up Reckless' training, getting her comfortable with the heavy, rigid contraption on her back, first alone and then, incrementally, with shells strapped on. He would have walked her, and then jogged her, first on level ground, then up and down hills. Chances are he would have loaded her with more shells than he planned on her carrying, so that her routine load would seem easier, but also knowing that there would be times he would have to ask more of her, perhaps a lot more. Just as Latham had given Reckless time to get accustomed to her surroundings, and become attached to her Marines and they to her, so he paced this phase of her training.

They had a month in reserve camp, which suited his careful, gentle approach. It was much the way he watched her diet—never spoiling the guys' fun in feeding her the mess hall chow she loved, but making sure she got proper horse food when he could. Riding her, too. He let guys take a turn on her, but not all the time and, as best he could manage, allowing only the lighter ones to ride.

By late January 1953, when the Fifth Regiment went back on line, Reckless had made corporal. Her training now was on the job, and already it seemed like she understood what was being asked of her. Even on the first runs, as Latham or one of her other buddies would accompany her from the ammunition depot to the recoilless rifle she was supplying, when they reached the bottom of the designated hill, with an encouraging "Up you go, gal," she would move out, hitting her own stride. Negotiating the twisting trail and rocky footing with ease, she emerged from the cover of scrub growth to a waiting member of the fire squad anxious for the shells. No matter how heated the fighting, they made time for words of praise and a neck rub.

An unexpected incident made the Marines realize just how solid a horse she was. As Guy Wagoner remembered it, "I'd just brought a truckload of shells up from Headquarters Company, and I'd climbed up on the ridge to tell everyone the ammo was here. Reckless was already there, standing with one of the guys near the recoilless rifle, saddled up and waiting to start hauling shells.

"Our planes had made a strike on the North Korean line. Evidently, one of them had made a really good hit because it was coming our way, the pilot moving his ailerons and doing a little victory roll. It was one of those Corsairs, the planes they mostly used for close air support.

"Damned if one of his napalm canisters didn't fly off. We all just froze. It hit about 40 feet the other side of the gun," Wagoner said. The explosion rocked the ridge. It was just luck that the canister hit on its outer edge, and the blast blew away from the Marines and Reckless. She pranced a little and let out a couple of disapproving whinnies, nothing more. "My God, what a horse," he added. "It was hard to imagine one being that stable." Wagoner headed back to the States soon thereafter, sure in his own mind that his friend, "Pete" Pedersen, had made the right call.

The exploding canister may have frayed a few nerves that day, but the guys on the ridge also knew they had one less target to worry about. Close air support was a much-lauded Marine contribution in the Korean War that enabled pilots to fly low, guided in for a pinpoint attack by forward observers on the ground. The low-level bombings, sometimes from only 100 feet above an enemy target, meant that pilots could strike enemy pockets close to U.N. forces with such precision that mostly they avoided deaths by friendly fire, unlike what could happen with payloads dropped from much higher altitudes.

2

The focus of why Reckless was with the Marines—the 75mm recoilless rifle—was developed at the end of World War II, too late for it to see much use in that conflict. But once the Korean War morphed into trench warfare roughly along the 38th Parallel, the recoilless rifle found its calling—and the enemy had a nemesis. The weapon could destroy a bunker, a pillbox, a cave, or other enemy personnel target—the kind of targets that smaller weapons could not dislodge—with tremendous accuracy from two or three miles away. Its maximum firing range was 7,000 yards, giving it a piercing capability over the longest distance of anything in the war other than artillery. It used three types of shells, weighing 20.5 pounds to almost 23 pounds. Normally, rounds of HE or high explosives were fired at a target first, followed by a round of smoke or white phosphorus to burn out what was inside. If the target was a tank or other armored vehicle, a third type of shell, HEAT (High Explosive Anti-Tank) was used.

The rifle itself was an imposing 115 pounds and measured six feet, ten inches. It, too, was hauled up the hills, and back down when the mission was over. They could break it apart into three sections to transport, but mostly it was moved as a single piece—by four men each grabbing a handle or, more likely, just two men. If they were different heights and arm lengths, it complicated the uphill haul, and there were times one guy hefted the rifle on his shoulder and made the climb by himself. The gunner ran ahead with the tripod, setting it up on the ridge, ready for the others to lock on the barrel. After Reckless came on line, some of the weapons went up the hill with her—the barrel strapped on one side of her saddle, counterbalanced by the tripod and two or three shells on the other side.

The crew had no choice but to work in the open since the recoilless rifle, as a direct-fire weapon, sent its shell in a straight path toward its target. Firing it from the cover of the reverse slope, as could be done with mortars, would have blown the top of the ridgeline off. But with no cover, the huge back blast of white smoke that was discharged with each firing fanned out for some 30 feet. Belching from the rear of the barrel, it could easily injure, even kill someone slammed by its thrust. The smoke lingered on the ridge, and along with each blast gave away the rifle's location. Within minutes the returning fire started. A recoilless rifle could do enormous damage and the enemy wanted to knock it out if it possibly could.

After every few rounds—usually four, at most five—the guys were on the move, grabbing the recoilless rifle with tripod attached, the shells, and Reckless, and running a quarter mile up the line to their next position. That was the routine, keeping on the move. In their wake, like as not, they left an aggravated group—Marines firing other weapons—whose positions, even in trenches or on the reverse slope of the hill had also been identified.

"We used to yell at them," said Staff Sergeant Jack Nelmark, from Wausau, Wisconsin, who headed a mortar squad for Fox Company, Second Battalion, Fifth Regiment. "We were out doing what we do, and here come the recoilless guys. We knew what would happen, we were going to draw more fire because of them. Any forward observer with the Chinese could see exactly where they were from that puff of smoke. So it wasn't long after they started firing that the incoming would begin." Nelmark and his crew headed for a bunker. "Hell, we weren't going to stand around. We'd get killed."

Nevertheless, the value of the recoilless rifle in hilly-to-mountainous Korea was beyond debate. The Recoilless Rifle Platoon, essentially a floater unit, went where it was needed. As a part of a regimental company, it was available to support any of the regiment's three battalions and their companies, depending on what units were on line and their combat assignments. When the recoilless rifles could assist, they were called in. Frequently, they fired on targets of opportunity—those being targets that were unplanned or unanticipated—that could be taken out by the rifle's straight trajectory.

"It could have been a case when the Chinese were giving us a rough time," explained Sergeant Jack Railo, "and we'd call up Pedersen's men to blow out one of their bunkers." Railo, from Brighton, Massachusetts, was a machine gunner and section leader, also with Fox Company, Second Battalion, Fifth Regiment. It was always a daylight mission, given that the recoilless rifle's target had to be visible. The squads would set up on the ridge before sunrise. "Then, as there was enough light to pick out their targets, they would begin firing on them," Railo added.

Besides the Fifth, three other infantry regiments—the First and Seventh—were in Korea, each organized the same, and each with its own Recoilless Rifle Platoon. There was also an artillery regiment, the Eleventh, and the First Korean Marine Regiment, the latter set up, equipped, and trained with the assistance of the U.S. Marine Corps. They all belonged to the Corps' First Division, the only Marine division serving in the Korean War. Not just the 75mm recoilless rifles, but all the weapons in the war came out of previous conflicts—namely World War II or, in some cases, models from World War I retooled for World War II. From the M1 rifle to the Browning Automatic Rifle, to mortars and machine guns, to .45-caliber pistols and .30-caliber carbines, they were what had been used or intended for use in those earlier conflicts. With few exceptions, the same was true of artillery and armor—rockets, howitzers, and tanks. The Marines in Korea, it was said, used weapons of World War II to fight a conflict reminiscent of the trench warfare of World War I.

—— **3** ——

As a member of the regiment, Reckless now did her part to defend the Jamestown Line, the Marine-controlled section of the Main Line of Resistance (MLR). When the recoilless rifle squads went out, routinely she was taken along whether they were on patrol for targets or when their firepower had been specifically requested. How many shells she carried to the gun positions was a matter of opinion. Some of the guys remembered four, others six, making some combination of those numbers likely. But Reckless' legend is strong, and others were sure she packed ten shells or more. What is true, at least, is that Jeju ponies were (and still are) remarkably tough little animals, beyond what their size would suggest.

She was definitely a thorn in the enemy's side. The opposition, mostly Chinese by the winter of 1953, wanted her eliminated—and they looked for opportunities to do just that. Railo recounted a morning when they put an end to one such attempt. He and some of the guys from his section were on the ridge before daybreak when they zeroed in on a Chinese gunner on the opposing forward slope. They had seen him before.

"He always used to aggravate us, putting rounds in the air," Railo recalled. The Chinese gunner would purposely aim fire behind the line, and some of the incoming would land in Reckless' paddock, a half mile back. "The poor horse would be running around, trying to stay clear of the shrapnel and get to her bunker."

That morning they had enough, and called in the recoilless rifle guys. "They came up on the ridge, watched him until he'd worked his way closer, and they put a round right in the guy's face. Yeah, they blew him to pieces," said Railo. "I mean, it was a sorry thing to say, but to heck with him and good luck to us."

To keep Reckless safe on line, when they had a choice they would have her supply recoilless rifles that were set up near some tree cover. It gave the guys a place to keep her out of sight when she wasn't working. Some days she supplied two rifles at a time—which, not surprisingly, annoyed the fire squads who didn't get her help and had to haul their own shells.

"The guys next to us, they had 90 percent of Reckless. And here our squad had to carry all our own ammo, and we didn't think that was fair," recalled Doug Christopherson about one combat operation. "We kept talking about that. You know, 'How come those guys got that horse to do all their heavy work?'" They knew it was because the guys next to them on the hill were in a more protected area, and Reckless wouldn't be so apt to get hit. Still, once everyone saw how much ammunition she could move, they wanted her help.

"She was pretty salty," was Chuck Batherson's take after watching her during a fire mission. He and the Tankers were some distance down the ridge, and he had his binoculars on her. "They were getting incoming and, sure, I could see that she was moving around some. But she didn't run, didn't even try," he recalled. "She got hit that day, too. A little nick. "No matter what happened, never once did I hear any of the guys say Reckless ran. She might have been scared, but she stayed. She was there."

They saw that the first time she hauled shells to the ridge. Even then, standing near a blasting recoilless rifle, she held her ground better than anyone could have hoped. Latham had used the platoon's previous time on line, in the fall of 1952, to acclimate her to what she would be dealing with. Likely, he trailered her near the ridge, walked her around rice paddies, calmed her when incoming started and there was no bunker accessible to them, and brought her close to the sounds she had never heard in reserve camp. It was a careful plan, and it paid off.

Coming up to the ridge in late January 1953, in the midst of a firefight, Latham did not have the luxury of choosing a good time for their arrival.

The guns needed shells and now Reckless was on the job. No sooner had she stepped into the clearing than the recoilless rifle let loose, sending its blast of firepower across a valley and its back blast across the ridge. Latham held firm to her halter, not sure what to expect. He stroked her neck, but whatever he said to her was drowned out by the roar.

In an instant, Reckless was airborne, all four feet off the ground. The weight on her back seemed like nothing as she jumped. Her eyes grew huge, her ears flicked back and forth. She landed, but within seconds another blast tore out of the rifle. This time only her front feet pawed the air. With the third blast, she pranced a little, all four feet on the ground. Then one more blast, the fourth—all of this within a couple of minutes— and there she was, her head down, her lips working across the ground, searching for something to eat. Some shook their heads in disbelief, others sighed with relief. A good bet, there were smiles all around.

It was a big step forward, and it could have been otherwise. The horse's fight and flight response could have kicked in. Reckless could have been spooked at the noise and smoke, spun around on her haunches and raced back down the hill, around the rice paddy, and off to who knows where. It could have been a catastrophe and, at least for a first try, an indication that her future hauling shells to the recoilless rifles might not work out.

Then what would become of Reckless? Would the platoon keep her? Would there be another job she could do? Could she stay on as their mascot? In truth, as much as she had already won the affection of many of the guys, they could not ignore the fact that she was there for a particular reason. But so far, their worries were groundless. She had done everything they asked of her.

—— 4 ——

Remembering Reckless years later, her Marine buddies often expressed awe, even amazement at how she fit right into the platoon, and what she was able to accomplish. How was it all possible, they wondered? Was Reckless a fluke, an anomaly that was able to perform in an extraordinary manner? Or was the explanation simpler, rooted in the skills of two horsemen—Pedersen, the rancher, and Latham, the farmer—who understood how her fundamental reactions and instincts could be tailored to fit her new environment and the tasks at hand?

That was the thinking of Dr. Robert Miller, the renowned large animal veterinarian and equine behaviorist, from Thousand Oaks, California. Without knowing any of the details of her story, he was convinced that Reckless had been handled by very capable people who clearly had the temperament and experience to work with her. What she and Joe Latham, her primary trainer, had accomplished suggested nothing less.

Miller was beginning his veterinary practice at the same time Reckless was proving her mettle in the Korean War, and it was many years before he heard about her. It came by way of a revelation from his good friend, Harold Wadley, a rancher from St. Maries, Idaho. Wadley had been in Korea, with Weapons Company, Third Battalion, Fifth Regiment, and remembered Reckless working under some fearsome conditions. Through many years of ranching thereafter, he bred some exceptionally fine horses, yet he surprised Miller by telling him that she was the best horse he had ever known.

Hearing Reckless' story, Miller understood. Horses, like people, have variable temperaments, and Reckless came to the Marines with an admirable one, Miller believed. She was intelligent, able to rapidly grasp what was being asked of her, and she quickly became conditioned to new, often frightening situations. The attributes gave her an edge over any number of other horses, yet beyond that, what was achieved was due to a perfect confluence of factors. She was not, as Miller was quick to point out, a freak of nature.

Reckless had what some horsemen will call a yielding personality, which was apparent in her quick willingness to accept her new family. In nature, horses choose to live in groups, as do other familiar species like cattle, sheep, and dogs. Only cats are comfortable loners and even among them, lions and their prides are an exception. All of them, to be sure, prefer the company of their own kind. Watching horses intermingling in a field—grazing, grooming each other, moving about—shows how strong the need is for companionship and to be part of a herd. It doesn't matter if it is three or three hundred, horses thrive with company.

Psychologically, having companionship is so important that horses will accept surrogates when their own kind is not available. On the racetrack, a donkey may share a horse's stall, or a rabbit or rooster will be in a cage close enough for a horse to rub its nose against. In Reckless' case, she left behind her racetrack family who, even in war-torn Seoul, would have looked upon their horses as the center of their world. In their place, she inherited a platoon of Marines who showered her with affection, from the day she arrived on base. Neither the racetrack nor the Marines was a natural group for her to adopt, but judging by Reckless' easy acceptance of life with the Marines, she had been well treated before and was willing to trust her new family.

Not every member of the platoon fussed over her. There were some for whom Reckless held no particular attraction, and who barely noticed her. But it was a neutral reaction—never mean-spirited in any way, simply passive. The guys who interacted with

Reckless always treated her in a kind and positive manner. They became her herd but, unlike behavior typical in a herd of horses, there was no fight for dominance, no sorting out of leaders and followers, no pecking order to be accepted. With her buddies around, she felt safe and secure. It could not have been better—an affectionate, caring, supportive herd. Or as Miller said, "The perfect herd."

In her way, Reckless understood that Joe Latham was her boss— in equine terms, the herd leader. If it was on Jeju Island where she was foaled, an older mare would likely have been in charge of the herd, telling Reckless and the other ponies what to do. When danger was imminent, the mare would have led the flight, the others running behind her and a stallion bringing up the rear. She embodied experience, her efforts to keep the herd safe bred trust. Latham built the same connection with Reckless, and what she gave back followed from there. Like he always said, "Treat animals well and they'll do anything for you."

What was sure about Reckless' life before she joined the Marines was that from the time she was a year old or so, it is safe to say, her days were hardly tranquil. If she came from Jeju Island in the fall of 1950, with the ponies acquired by the Korean Racing Authority to replenish their lost stock and be ready whenever racing resumed, she wound up living through the last two battles for Seoul. Reckless would have been part of the racing community that gravitated back to what was left of the racetrack, though it is unclear how close the track was to the fighting, when the enemy retook the capital in January 1951, and the U.N. forces liberated it two months later. But in the spring of 1951, when the racetrack became an airstrip, she learned to live with the daily sounds of airplanes taking off and landing, and her ability to cope with that was obvious by the calm and tractable horse Pedersen found.

Every new stimulus—that is, one that the horse has never heard or seen before—can be a potential problem. That Reckless coped or, to be more accurate, became desensitized to airplane engines was certainly a good indication of what she was capable, but the recoilless rifle was a separate issue. She needed to come within feet of it, so that she would hear, see, and feel the enormous blast. The guys on the fire squad crouched, covered their ears, and turned their backs when the gun fired. Reckless would have to come to terms with it in her own way.

As long as it doesn't cause pain, an animal can become completely indifferent to the loudest, most frightening sound. The process of desensitizing, also called habituating, occurs automatically with careful repetition. By repeating the same stimulus, in Miller's experience 25 to 50 times depending on the animal's temperament, the information that a particular stimulus is non-threatening is filed away in the animal's memory bank for future recall. The horse's concern over that stimulus is put to rest. And said Miller, "Their memory is infallible."

What makes the horse so incredibly useful, and from which all hopes spring for its future, is a hand-in-glove occurrence that is extraordinary in its import. Desensitizing an animal curbs the flight response and is what makes them tractable. As a grazing animal, horses are prey to attack, and flight is their defense and protection. But taken to the extreme, if everything frightened them, they would never stop running, never take time to eat, sleep, or reproduce. Given their ability to become desensitized, however, once a horse determines that a stimulus is not dangerous, its flight response can be harnessed. Each stimulus is a separate challenge, but each one that the horse recognizes as non-threatening makes the next one easier to accept.

Still, a war setting is far from ideal as a training ground, and in the environment that Reckless and her Marines found themselves, understandably, the process of desensitizing was harder to control than elsewhere. Circumstances varied, other sounds intruded—napalm explosions, automatic rifle and mortar fire, along with the recoilless rifle blasts—and with it all, she absorbed what she needed to know. Latham had put the parts together seamlessly—her buddies, the sights and sounds of the front line, the saddle, the shells, the weapon and then, finally, bringing Reckless up on the ridge to stand near the recoilless rifle being fired. The flight response—leaping into the air, pawing with her front legs, shying—diminished with each blast. After the third shell was fired, Reckless understood that the rifle would not hurt her, and with the fourth blast, any lingering doubts were put to rest. Said Miller, "Unusual, but perfectly understandable."

Once they saw Reckless' response under fire, Pedersen and Latham pushed the envelope. They needed more from her, specifically that she traverse the route between the ammunition depot and the ridgeline alone. The memories of this lone pony, circling the rice paddies and climbing the hills by herself carried a secret. As she stopped at the end of each crossing, a food treat awaited—surely encouragement for one who loved food as much as she did. What had transpired, Miller explained, was that Latham would have accompanied Reckless at least three times between the two points, feeding her at the top of the hill and when she returned to the depot. "She was going to keep seeking that reward," he explained, as to why she continued to travel on her own.

Moving between the two points, guys remembered Reckless' savvy in being able to protect herself when incoming hit the area. She would perk up her ears at the first sounds, then go to the side of the nearest hill and push up against it, trying to flatten herself and get out of the way. Experience had already told her that the sound meant shells were going to land someplace, and where she was she didn't have a bunker to take cover in.

Her instincts about the rifle itself needed sharpening, however. No one could predict, in an intense firefight, what it would be like on the ridge. Someone was usually watching for Reckless, and would be quick enough to take hold of her when she arrived. But there could be those few moments when everyone's eyes were elsewhere. She was desensitized to the firing, but was she smart enough to keep from getting herself caught in the back blast? It was routine for her to be stopped and her cargo unloaded several feet from the rifle, but Latham still trained her to always come up to the barrel at right angles and midpoint to its length.

Maybe learning the hard way was the best lesson. A couple of times, Latham and Reckless approached the rifle close to the rear of the barrel as it was discharging. "Yeah, we got caught in the back blast," Latham admitted. "I brought her in on too small an angle to the rear, and the power of that thing caught us and knocked us down." Perhaps because her boss was with her, and both of them scrambled to their feet, she took a cue from his reaction--startled, probably a little shaken, but nothing worse. The knockdowns must have taught Reckless something. At least, nothing more adverse was ever reported.

——— 5 ———

Little changed as the New Year began. The war in January 1953 was about the same as it had been for the past two months. The temperature sank to frigid levels and the fighting cooled down. Engagements continued—aggressive patrols, raids, limited objective attacks—but only a few were significant and no real estate changed hands. The Marines kept the outposts within No Man's Land that they had fortified, and the Chinese kept theirs.

Along the length of the MLR, more than 150 miles from coast to coast, thousands of rounds of fire were exchanged daily between the two sides. For the time being there were no grand offensives but, just the same, casualties mounted and lives were lost.

President-Elect Dwight D. Eisenhower fulfilled a campaign promise to go to South Korea, secretly flying there in early December 1952. His victory over Adlai Stevenson had been a landslide, and he saw it as a mandate to end the war as quickly as possible. The few days he spent at the front, talking with commanders and meeting enlisted men, made it clear to him that for U.N. forces to remain on a static front, sustaining casualties without meaningful results, could not continue open-ended. Through some combination of diplomacy and military pressure, the hostilities had to be stopped.

Frustrating the U.N. side, the peace talks were still stalled. Whatever the behind-the-scenes efforts, they had yet to bring the participants back to the meeting tables at Panmunjom. The principal sticking point was what to do with prisoners of war, specifically the many North Koreans who did not want to go home.

In February, the Marines turned the heat up. Colonel Lewis Walt, the new commander of the Fifth Regiment, set into motion plans for two raids on Un-Gok, a huge land mass about six miles east of the Peace Corridor and a half mile north of the front line. It was actually four hills, like all of them designated by numbers, but only the specialists referred to them that way. The first raid, Operation Clambake, was undertaken by Able Company, First Battalion. With the Recoilless Rifle Platoon in support, Reckless got her first taste of full-scale combat.

The Chinese were dug in all along the Marines' Western Front, and that included Un-Gok's high ground. Un-Gok opened the way to Seoul and if the enemy had any hope of reinvading South Korea, it was ground they had to hold. Operation Clambake, the Marines' plan to retake the hills, went forward on February 3. The temperature was below zero.

Operations had varying agendas, from taking prisoners and gaining intelligence to outright destruction, and this one was to be the latter— destroy the enemy and all his positions. Undertaken in daylight, the operation supported Able Company with air attacks, flame-throwing tanks, artillery, and the 75mm recoilless rifles. It achieved its objective, but the enemy's stronger-than-expected resistance was a warning of what could develop.

The Marines kept up the pressure, launching a succession of smaller raids through the month. Then at first light on February 25, the Fifth Regiment took the blueprint for Operation Clambake and set in motion Operation Charlie. The target, another couple of miles east, was Outpost Detroit, which had been in Chinese hands since they overran it the previous October. The Marines did not want the hill back, but they did want to give it and its occupants a good pounding. This time Fox Company, Second Battalion took the lead.

Reckless again supported the recoilless fire squads, hauling her cargo of shells across 300 yards of open rice paddies before reaching Detroit's base. Presumably, in a later recap from a proud Lieutenant Pedersen, it was reported that she carried more than 3,500 pounds of shells, traveling some 20 miles back and forth from the ammunition depot to the front line. For a battle that was over by early morning, the amount of ammunition Reckless delivered to the ridge was nothing less than a feat of speed and endurance.

Nevertheless, Colonel Walt and his staff were not satisfied with the intelligence. Their gut reaction told them the Chinese were up to something, and they wanted another crack at

Un-Gok. Three weeks later, Baker Company, First Battalion, jumped off in the short, intense Operation Item, this time with the goal to take prisoners and gain more information.

Scout Sergeant Jim Larkin, from Rockaway Beach in Queens, New York, was a member of Baker Company's Forward Observer Team. The recoilless rifles, he remembered, were set up about 30 yards to the right of the company. "They were continuously firing, which meant they were using a lot of ammo. Reckless was a pretty busy mare," he said. "We were occupied ourselves, and I didn't have time to go over and say, 'Hello, Reckless'. But she was there, that amazing little horse.

"The amount of ammo she carried up to the line while they were firing made an enormous difference," he added, pointing out how many men and how much longer it would have taken to get the shells to the ridge without her.

The Fifth Marines prevailed, pushing the Chinese off Un-Gok's high ground. But within two days, the enemy challenged the First Marines on Outposts Esther and Hedy, both of them within three miles west of Un-Gok. Though the Chinese expended considerable firepower, they failed to crack the U.N. front line.

6

Reckless was an unusual warhorse, not in size, which in her part of the world was not uncommon, but in the role she was given and that she expanded for herself. She was not among hundreds or thousands charging into battle, her rider's legs urging her on, the reins slapping at her neck. Nor was she hitched into a line of packhorses, hauling a heavy piece of artillery to its firing position, or even a single packhorse being lead by a mounted horse. Neither a rider nor the movements of other horses signaled to her what to do. In Reckless' case, when it was asked of her, it meant going it alone, calling on heightened abilities that reflected the best of what horses can do. One of a kind, who can say? A standout, who marched to her own drummer, there is no question.

Horses were sent to war thousands of years before Reckless came on the scene. Once they were domesticated, their participation in battle was a foregone conclusion, supported by a simple equation: warriors on foot were no match for a foe charging them on horseback. From there, the horse's role expanded over the millennia, predominantly as a cavalry mount and supply train, until finally horses lost place to mechanization.

The earliest mounted warriors, first recorded about 5,000 B.C., were the Mongols who invaded China on their tough, little ponies, as a benefit introducing the Mongolian horse to China. Unlike the Mongols, however, who continued to ride their horses, the Chinese were early users of horse-drawn chariots from which warlords did battle, besides employing horses as cavalry mounts. Of course, Reckless herself descended from one of the early warhorses. Then as now, the smallest of the East Asian breeds, the indigenous Korean pony, thousands of years before it took the name Jeju, was a recorded participant in wars on the Korean Peninsula beginning in the third century B.C.

Mostly, nations continued to build on the capabilities of the mounted warrior, raising huge cavalries and developing different types of horses: warmbloods for riding, and coldbloods for draught and pack work. The Assyrians, Scythians, Persians, Romans, and Saracens all waged wars with massive cavalries, though nothing could compare to Ogtai Khan's one and a half million horses with riders, the largest cavalry in recorded history, that swept across Eastern Europe as far as Poland in the 12th century A.D.

Meanwhile, in Europe a new style of cavalry emerged using larger horses to carry armor-clad knights. Frequently the horses were covered in their own armor, as well, and together with the weight of their rider could be asked to carry as much as 400 pounds. Such displays of pageantry and power would have been dramatically presented in the early 15th century, when King Henry V of England sailed for France with a war-ready armada that contained as many as 25,000 horses. Their numbers were doled out according to social rank: 50 horses for a duke, 24 for an earl, six for a knight, four for an esquire, and one for a horse archer.

Yet, by the end of the 15th century, the advent of firearms foreshadowed another type of cavalry horse. Swift death to the enemy from gunpowder replaced a battering death from charging knights on horseback, and relieved the horse of much of the weight that had been imposed on him. By the latter 17th century, faster, lighter English Thoroughbreds—a cross of English and Arabian breeds—began refining the cavalry, driving the concept of using specific types of horses for particular needs: small, solid horses for transporting foot soldiers to another battle site; light, fast horses for sudden, quick attacks; and strong, powerful horses for the galloping charges.

Though its battle capabilities changed, the use of the cavalry and its horses continued unabated, and always with a dismal, gut-wrenching side. Of the 30,000 cavalry horses, and likely as many pack and draught horses, that Napoleon took to Russia in 1812, during the Napoleonic Wars, fewer than 2,000 survived the Cossacks' savagery. And while Alfred, Lord Tennyson immortalized a terrible disaster in a popular epic poem, *The Charge of the Light Brigade*, the reality in the Battle of Balaclava, in 1854, during the Crimea War, was that the misdirected British cavalry rushed headlong into the firing Russian artillery. The dreadful imbalance of artillery against the slashing blade left nearly 300 men dead and close to double that number of horses.

America had established a cavalry under the Department of the

Army in 1777, though it was many years before it truly came into its own. Not until the westward expansion began in earnest in the early 1800s, and later during the Civil War, did the cavalry gain a prominent role. In the latter half of the 1800s, as the wave of westbound settlers reached its zenith, an expanded cavalry continued to face the inflamed Indian tribes being displaced in the many Indian Wars. Superb Indian horsemen on their surefooted Mustangs, however, found themselves no match for the improving weaponry on the side of settlers and their protectors.

Worldwide, the warhorse's presence in military conflicts would remain undiminished for another half century. The battlefield grew increasingly uneven as advances in weaponry confronted outdated tactics. Yet, with the world not sufficiently mechanized, the horse stayed—serving in the South African Wars; with Theodore Roosevelt and his Rough Riders in Cuba; in conflicts in Mexico, the Philippines, the Far East, and elsewhere, into the early 20th century.

The U.S. Marines mounted up their own cavalry for a short period in the 1900s. In an eclectic mix of assignments, the U.S. Marine Corps Horse Marines were present in Ethiopia, Haiti, and the Banana Wars in Central America. Best known, however, were the China Marines, mounted units which served in China from 1909 to 1938, guarding the American Embassy in Peking (Beijing) and the International Settlement in Shanghai.

It remained for one last major conflict, World War I, to rely on horses as vital partners in the conduct of battle. And though it is dimming now, World War I was part of the world's collective memory, giving people a sense as never before of the brutality of war and, indeed, a warhorse's life. The numbers needed were staggering. By mid-war, the British Army, by itself, was using more than half a million horses and another quarter million mules. In the first two years of the conflict, the U.S. contributed one million horses to the European forces, and after entering the war in 1917, brought nearly 200,000 additional horses for its own battle use.

Part of the plight was that few horses returned to their homes. Perhaps the enormity of their numbers deployed to the many fronts—as cavalry mounts, and pack and draught animals—and the appalling survival rates, made their exit from war even more laudable as, by the end of World War I, mechanization became sufficient to take over the horses' work. Horse cavalries made a limited contribution in World War II—primarily in Russia, Germany, and Poland, and as packhorses in the mountainous regions of Italy and the jungles of Burma—but the horse's role as a major player in waging war was over.

Their long and extraordinary contribution, of course, was because horses have functioned well in war. All the attributes that Reckless exhibited—the ease with which she was desensitized, her willingness to accept surrogate company, her physicality, her steadiness—made many horses excellent choices for the right task. While horses were not officially issued to the U.N. forces in the Korean War, their presence suggested that when they became available, they were a welcome asset.

There was no question that horses and mules were used by both sides. For the U.N. forces, it was mostly North Korean stock that got loose and was captured by individual units. Given the rugged terrain, virtually all the animals that were taken, if they were in decent shape, were kept and used as packhorses. In a postwar report, the U.S. Army Quartermaster Corps said that, while anecdotal, instances of animals used by U.S. military units filled several pages. Those who had horses were reluctant to admit to any particulars—the numbers or where they came from—for fear that their use would be prohibited, or the animals would be moved elsewhere.

The enemy's use of packhorses was well known. Corporal Mark Marquette, from Chicago, Illinois, routinely picked up their presence on night patrols, when he was a forward observer with the Eleventh Regiment. Enemy troops would be moving along a ridge, maybe half a mile away, as Marquette described it, crawling in supplies with the help of horses. "Then they would vanish into the valley behind," he said. "And the next day we would pull a horse to safety on our side, presumably one that had been separated from his group the night before."

U. N. forces also picked up horses from those bands of ponies that were sent careening from North Korean hills across No Man's Land to the Allied positions. Those that made it across alive, and it seemed most did, were kept or dispersed to other units. At some point, one of them even found shelter with the Fifth Regiment's Recoilless Rifle Platoon, one Marine remembered. He was a rougher, thicker-boned pony than Reckless—and outside of her spotlight, apparently noticed by very few.

As far as anyone knew, among all the horses in the Korean War, Reckless was the only one to gain fame. She was known up and down the Marine line and, little being sacred, the object of expected wisecracks, to wit:

"Hey, did you hear? The Fifth has a horse," the opener.

"Oh, yeah, sure it isn't a cow?" the reply.

The Fifth was ripe for a ribbing, and no one was going to miss the chance.

————— **7** —————

Forward camp, for the two months at a stretch that the regiment spent on line, was about basics. Sleeping quarters came in two types—four-man tents, pitched on the incline of a hill facing away from the enemy or, for more security, sandbag- and log-reinforced bunkers. The latter were dug into the walls of trenches, that meandering string of ditches, usually five to seven feet deep that cut across the front line hills. To give themselves more protection, Marines also dug fighting holes in the trench walls outside the bunkers.

Some days, hot food packed in insulated containers was trucked up from field kitchens. More often, Marines got the day's meals, an assortment of C-rations, in a single cardboard box. The contents included canned foods like sausage patties in gravy, corned beef hash, or franks and beans, all of which could be heated over a can of Sterno. There was also canned fruit, cookies, crackers, candy, instant coffee, and cigarettes. Reckless liked everything, including the cigarettes, preferably when the packs were opened.

The guys did the best they could for her, but forward camp was as tough on Reckless as it was on her buddies, and the stress was evident. She dropped weight, and with her dirty, matted coat, she looked as grubby as everyone else. For her safety, they had to keep her in a paddock, spacious as it was, and at night they barricaded her in her bunker. She had visitors whenever there was a quiet day or a break in the action. The guys brought her whatever food they could—grasses they pulled, grains if they could get some, and always items from their own rations. She hungered for their attention and they were happy to give it.

Reckless' bond with her buddies had deepened. Although they were surrogates for her own kind, she had accepted them as her herd. As they behaved, she behaved. Their reactions were hers, as well. They stood their ground despite their own fears and, seeing that, the cue to her was to stay put. Latham or one of his stand-ins was telling her, in effect, that there was no danger for her to run from, reinforcing the desensitization to the blast of the recoilless rifle and other sights and sounds of combat. Even when she was traveling alone from the ammunition depot to the rifle positions, she was moving between members of the herd. At each end it was someone she knew who had her treat waiting, and that overruled any desire to run away.

On tough workdays like the ones involving operations Clambake, Charlie, and Item, the guys paced Reckless as much as they could, giving her periodic breaks for water and feed, pulling the saddle off and toweling her down, then checking her over, particularly her legs, to make sure she hadn't scraped herself in the underbrush as she plowed through it. She was hauling four to six shells, at a top weight of over 120 pounds, and once unloaded, ran down the hill for more. At day's end she was exhausted, but she kept going as long as she was needed.

The spring thaw had begun, the runoff from melting snow and ice turning the roads into muck and the trenches into mud holes. Miles south, the Imjin River was starting to churn, as the ice floes broke apart, crashed into each other and headed downriver, speeding up the current.

As the temperature rose, there were signs that the war was heating back up. At the end of March, the Fifth Regiment held the principal combat outposts at the eastern edge of the Marine Sector—East Berlin, Berlin, Vegas, Reno, Carson, and Ava. The First Regiment held Esther, Hedy, Bunker Hill, Dagmar, and Ginger, among others, and the Korean Marines held on to still others. The Seventh Regiment was in reserve. Intelligence reports indicated that the Chinese had other ideas about who should occupy what outposts and they were planning to make some changes.

What the Marines on the line knew, however, was that the Fifth Regiment would be heading back to reserve camp very soon. They were ready. Another month and they would be wading through slop, and nobody wanted to hang around the front for that. Clean clothes and hot showers were on everyone's minds, plus Reckless could get some rest. She had done her part, showed what she was made of. What she needed was good food, time to wander around and hang out with her buddies, and a good sudsing with soap and hot water.

Just a few more days.

Except on March 26, 1953, all hell broke loose, and reserves were canceled.

Chapter Four

ONE EXTRAORDINARY HORSE

—— 1 ——

It had grown dark across the western slopes. A routine, warmer-than-average day had seamlessly moved into a quiet early evening until, at precisely 7:00 p.m., the Chinese bombarded outposts from East Berlin to Hedy. Hurling everything they had in their arsenal, they opened fire with small arms, mortars, machine guns, and artillery. The attacks erupted without warning, battering Berlin, Vegas, Carson, Reno, Reno Block, Esther, Dagmar, and Bunker Hill, in addition to Hedy and East Berlin. Thursday, March 26, 1953, was the start of the worst Marine battle of the Korean War.

Ten minutes later the enemy poured off Un-gok, Arrowhead, and other hills in full force, 3,500 members of the 358th Chinese Regiment spreading across the Marines' sector to challenge each of the outposts. The imbalance was daunting. The attackers outnumbered those defending the outposts by many fold. Reno, Carson, and Vegas, it would become quickly apparent, took the brunt of the hellish assault. The other hills, located east and west of the key outposts, were diversions, pounded hard enough to keep everyone off kilter.

The main targets—Reno, Carson, and Vegas—were previously and, perhaps, more prosaically called Bruce, Allen, and Clarence. With the new names, the nickname of the Nevada Cities was a natural. The latter came by way of a comment from one Lieutenant Colonel Anthony Caputo, of the Second Battalion, Seventh Marine Regiment, who reportedly said, "Holding them will be a gamble." The remark would be prophetic.

No matter the challenge, the hills were coveted real estate. They formed a triangle, with each hill protected on its flanks by the other two. Collectively they offered prime viewing of the surrounding territory— valuable for the Marines who held them, wanted by the Chinese. The latter had tried to seize the outposts the previous fall, and now they were trying again.

In Marine hands, the outposts blocked the enemy's access to Seoul, some 30 miles south as the crow flies. More immediately, they guarded the U.N. Main Line of Resistance (MLR). If Reno, Carson, and Vegas fell, it would threaten the front line, and if that was breached the ramifications could change the outcome of the Korean War. Beyond those specifics, the enemy was always looking for additional land, no matter what size the take. It was the essence of the trench war. The enemy grabbed for more, the U.N. forces pushed back. However, what land was held by the enemy at the time the Armistice was signed would become part of North Korea.

From East Berlin to Hedy, the string of targets carried the acronyms OP or COP in front of each name, short for Outpost or Combat Outpost. They were designated hills in front of the U.N. main line, occupied and defended, and important for keeping tabs on the enemy, including tracking troop and supply buildups. The enemy had its share of outposts, as well, and the OPs for both sides co-mingled, sometimes fairly close together, within the irregular layout of No Man's Land.

The location of each of the Nevada Cities was to be especially important in the coming days. Carson was the most westerly of the three hills, and at less than a half mile from the front line was the closest of the outposts to the Marines' position. Reno, the apex of the triangle formed by the hills, was almost a mile from the MLR and, thus, very near the Chinese line. To the right of Reno, Vegas was about three-quarters of a mile from the MLR. It was the tallest hill and had the best fields of observation. The three outposts were each manned around the clock by 40 to 50 Marines plus two Navy hospital corpsmen. Reno Block, also under attack, was a listening post manned at night only by a rifle squad. It was actually a little closer to the MLR than Carson and had excellent visibility—a fact that also worked to the enemy's advantage. Accordingly, when on Reno Block the guys had to puff on their cigarettes between cupped hands, so that the red glow could not be seen in the darkness.

As 1953 rolled out, the Chinese stayed fairly quiet unless prodded. They reacted to Marine incursions—the two attacks on Un-gok, Operations Clambake and Item, and between them, Operation Charlie against Outpost Detroit. And it was duly noted that the enemy's retaliatory power, the first time the Marines hit Un-gok, was stronger than had been expected. Essentially, the Chinese stance in the first three months of the year was to fight back when hit. On the one hand, there was little reason to complain about that; on the other hand, it was worrisome.

An entry in one of the Fifth Regiment command diaries offered the opinion that in winter the enemy was focused on keeping warm. With spring, it planned for military action, well aware of how much that season aggravated the Marines. Indeed, even though this would be their third spring in Korea, and the second in the Western Sector, familiarity would not make the outlook any brighter. To varying degrees, warming temperatures and melting snow brought a living and logistical mess—mud everywhere, difficulty in moving on foot and in vehicles, and the need to shore up trenches and bunkers weakened by previous bombarding, followed by too much water.

One way or another, the suspicion was that the Chinese were done with lying low. Something was about to blow a hole in the prevailing lull. But no one could have predicted the ferocity and brutality of the next five days. Nor could anyone have imagined the sheer guts of one small Korean pony named Reckless.

—— 2 ——

Sergeant Harold Wadley was one of the last people to get off Outpost Vegas before it was overrun or, as he put it, "The world turned upside down." A demolition expert—"zapper" was the term he used—Wadley moved around, working with whatever unit in the Fifth Regiment needed his help. That day, he had been with Howe Company, Third Battalion, blowing out caves, ironically so that there would be a place for the dead and wounded in the event of a heavy attack. Making his way back from Vegas to the main line, he could hear muffled coughing on both sides of the trail.

"It sounded like a sick cough to me, and I knew it wasn't our guys. Man, I high-tailed it and hollered at the gun gate that a Marine was coming in," he said, adding that he just made it through when the Chinese opened up with all manner of firepower. The enemy had let him pass rather than shoot him and blow its cover.

Age 17 and impatient to get to Korea, Wadley left his Oklahoma high school in the 11th grade and enlisted. "I asked the recruiter what kind of rifle I was going to get and how much ammo," he chuckled, explaining that he had some big shoes to fill. "A lot of my family fought in the trenches in World War I, and seven cousins and uncles fought in Europe and the Pacific in World War II."

With her son's promise that someday he would finish school—a promise he kept—his mother signed for him to join up. By the fall of 1952, Wadley was in combat.

For the first two and a half hours, that night of March 26, Marines up and down the line mounted a fierce defense. Of the Nevada Cities, Carson was hit first, then in quick succession, Reno and Vegas. Berlin and East Berlin were hammered and, to a lesser degree, the other outposts. By 9:30 p.m., the initial attack had ebbed some, as the enemy focused on the three hills they wanted. Because of its proximity to the MLR, the Marines were able to send reinforcements to Carson and hold it. But by midnight, five hours after the Chinese first attacked, Reno and Vegas were overrun and in enemy hands.

Their fall had come despite desperate attempts to push the attackers back. Reno especially, the farthest of the three outposts from the MLR, was difficult to reinforce. Platoons from Fox Company, Second Battalion, Fifth Regiment, were sent out one by one to try and reach the already battered platoon on Reno. It was not exactly what Jack Nelmark had in mind for that evening. The battalion had just gone into reserve, and the guys were set to relax and dig into their beer ration when the order came to move back up to the front.

"They began calling for more help up there on Reno. We were the closest ones, so we went. We had no idea how serious it was going to be," he recalled. "We were heading out there and they were already carrying out casualties. You start to think, 'Maybe this is the night I'm going to get hit.'"

Nelmark had been a drill instructor at Camp Pendleton, and was already a sergeant when, coming on base one day, he found out they needed some non-commissioned officers for the next replacement draft heading for Korea, and someone had signed him up. Arriving at Inchon in January 1953, on what he described as "a cold, foreboding day," he remembered the ship's captain saying, "Well, there you are, Marines, your home for the next year. Hope you like it."

Until the end of March, most of the action Nelmark saw was on patrols. They went out every night, for an hour or more—combat patrols, reconnaissance patrols. "Most of the time, nothing happened," he remembered. "But sometimes, we walked into an ambush, and all hell would break loose for about ten minutes. Then we'd pick up our dead and wounded and go back."

The night of March 26, however, turned a lot uglier, as the 60mm mortar crew he led tried to help their platoon move forward and break the enemy's lock on Reno. "I never figured I was going to get killed in Korea, no way. I had a wife and I was coming home," Nelmark said. "But that night the stuff was pouring in like rain. It felt like the Chinese wanted to get rid of all their ammo before the Armistice, and they were dumping it on our heads."

Nelmark's platoon moved off the MLR about 10:30 p.m. to reinforce another group that had gone ahead. Both were pinned down at Reno Block, the enemy's power so intense that the Marines could not advance any farther. Other units attempted to break through, but none could. Radio contact with Reno faltered, then went completely dead. The outpost was lost; the Marines who had occupied the summit were killed or taken prisoners. Outpost Vegas continued in play for a short time, its defenders fighting desperately to hold on. Then just before midnight, radio contact was broken and Vegas, too, was lost, all Marines on its summit also killed or captured.

With the first onslaught essentially over, Fifth Regiment Commander Lewis Walt was granted permission to pull all his troops back behind the MLR. Facing the enormity of the situation—a hugely disproportionate enemy strength and already high Marine casualties—in the parlance of the real Nevada cities, Colonel Walt rolled the dice. There would be a change in strategy. Realistically, too much ground had been lost to attempt to reclaim both outposts. They would not retake Reno but, instead, would neutralize it, destroying its installations with artillery fire and air strikes, so that the enemy could not use it as a staging area for troops and ammunition. That left Outpost Vegas, and the Marines would throw everything they had into getting it back.

Through the overnight hours, the Chinese turned their fire toward the main line, the 11th Regiment artillery continued to bombard Reno and Vegas, and the Marines set in motion a powerful counterattack. With Reno out of play, the First Battalion would continue to hold Carson, and the Second Battalion would assume the lead in retaking Vegas. Unfortunately, the sheer force of what had occurred before would repeat itself. The Marines' opening counterattack was met by several thousand Chinese.

---— 3 —---

Before daybreak on March 27, the recoilless rifle squads moved up on the ridgeline, ready to blast Vegas' summit and clear it for the advancing Marines. Reckless, in her paddock behind the reverse slope, would easily have picked up on the tension and heightened activity, likely reacting with some nervousness, and in need of a few extra hugs from her buddies to settle her down. It was probably Joe Latham or Monroe Coleman, another member of her inner circle, who took her on the introductory runs. Coleman's hometown of Loa was a tiny agricultural community in south-central Utah, and with his horse background, he, too, had cared for Reckless from the beginning. Now, they did what they had done in other combat situations. Talking to her and gesturing, they showed her where to walk and how best to scale the hill, meanwhile praying, as they always did, that she would make her journeys in safety.

The guys started carrying shells to the ridge. They didn't leave the stockpiling completely to Reckless, but as soon as she got going, her haul greatly overshadowed theirs, making her buddies proud. She had a tough route between the ammunition depot and the gun sites—across an open expanse of rice paddies, at one point a 45-degree climb to the ridge, and always the vulnerability to incoming fire. As in other combat situations, the rifles she supplied were high up and behind the mortar crews and riflemen, enabling them to fire overhead at targets that were impeding the ground assault.

Harold Wadley never forgot what Reckless went through. "She'd come away from the gun crew, along this little finger ridge, silhouetted as she moved. Then she would drop down on the back side of the ridge to where the ammo bunker was," he explained. "She was safe from direct fire there, but never, ever, out of the line of mortar and artillery fire, because that came over the top." The smells and the level of noise he called indescribable. "You couldn't hear yourself think, much less talk to someone beside you," he added, marveling at her steadiness through it all.

In the early morning of March 27, Marine artillery, planes flying close air support, mortars, and recoilless rifles pounded every enemy pocket that could be identified on and around Reno and Vegas. Then, blanketing the area with smoke, they set the stage and Dog Company, Second Battalion, Fifth Regiment, jumped off at 11:20 a.m., initiating the counterattack to retake Vegas. Efforts to advance met stiff resistance from the Chinese, and Dog Company began taking casualties. Easy Company, Second Battalion, Fifth Regiment and, later in the day, Fox Company, Second Battalion, Seventh Regiment, pressed the attack and by nightfall, some members had made it to Vegas' lower trenches. There they were stopped by the enemy, and by 8:30 that evening, Marines again withdrew to the MLR.

The Chinese still held Vegas' summit, its trenches and bunkers, but they were paying a terrible price, their casualties many times higher than those of the Marines. The indomitable warhorse of the Fifth Regiment could take some credit for that. In raw statistics, what she contributed in that first day of the battle for Outpost Vegas was beyond all expectations. The guys remember her always in motion, coming up to the gun site, being unloaded and heading back, never hesitating, never stopping save for the couple of times she was taken off her route for a snack and some rest.

Jim Larkin, who also got off Vegas in the nick of time, remembered the same look on Reckless' face that he had seen during Operation Clambake on the Un-gok hills. Whenever she came up on the ridge, he said, "There was almost a hint of impatience, as if she was saying, 'C'mon, let's go. Unload me, I've got to bring some more ammo up.'" Even the two wounds she sustained, both reportedly on her left side, one over her eye and the other on her flank, once treated did not slow her down. Indeed, it would be a source of pride for those who knew her, that on her dress blanket thereafter she wore two Purple Hearts.

Later, Lieutenant Pedersen put a fine point on that day with this accounting: Reckless made 51 trips from the ammunition depot to the recoilless rifle sites, traveling in all more than 35 miles. She carried 386 of the heavy shells, amounting to over 9,000 pounds of explosives. The gunners had enough ammunition that day that one of the rifles overheated from being fired so much.

With Reckless' workday over, her buddies took their weary horse back to her paddock, where she got dinner and a bucket of fresh water, a rubdown, and some much needed sleep. Could she have described her feelings, "bone-tired" would surely have said it all. But a long sleep was not in the cards. Whether or not someone said, "Sorry, gal," when they woke her up a few hours later is not known, of course. But as it turned out, Reckless was not just working days. At night, she was back on the job, hauling ammunition to the guys who were firing the mortars, struggling foot by foot to gain ground on Vegas. It is only an estimate, but with time out to eat and catch whatever sleep she could, she probably worked a good part of the three days and nights, March 27 through March 29, that it took to reclaim Vegas.

"I still see her on the skyline, in the giant flares. I just can't erase that image," said Wadley. "Those flare lights, dropped by planes, all that candlepower swinging down on parachutes, swinging and hissing, the lights and the shadows. And here's this little mare coming ahead." His voice trailed off. From a lifetime of working with horses, first farming and logging with them as a kid in Oklahoma, through all his years ranching in Idaho, he could offer no comparisons. "I don't think there was a warhorse in history, not another horse on the planet, that could do what Reckless did," he said.

She was battle worn, just like her buddies, and it showed. Wadley described her as being pretty trimmed down from the tough work and conditions, "and looking like she could pack on a lot more meat." Her Marines did everything possible for her, training her to keep her head down when there was incoming fire, and even covering her with their flak jackets, when they could. And always, they shared whatever they had to eat. "That included feeding her John Wayne cookies," he laughed, "those round, hard, C-ration crackers. We called them John Wayne cookies because you could hardly bite through them. The way we figured, nobody but Wayne was tough enough to eat one of them suckers." Wayne and Reckless, that was. She liked them just fine.

Nights, working forward of the MLR, Reckless again had to cross rice paddies, these between the main line and Vegas, to deliver ammunition to the mortar crews. The rounds were smaller and lighter and packaged differently than the recoilless rifle shells, and the guys had to figure out how to strap a number of boxes together and make the loads comfortable for her to carry. Jack Nelmark said that without the help she gave his crew, they would have run out of ammunition.

He would watch her come up to their forward line to be unloaded, "then they gave her a little slap on the butt and away she went," he said. The mines, they were everywhere, he remembered, yet somehow she never stepped on one. Coming across the rice paddies, she knew instinctively to stay on the narrow path, perhaps detecting an odor from the buried mines that warned her off. "If she had stepped on one, she would have detonated it with her weight, for sure," Nelmark added. "And she made the runs all by herself. But then, no one could keep up with her anyway. She was that fast."

Nelmark saw Reckless each of the three nights they fought for Vegas. Everyone knew she was a small pony, but to him she always seemed larger. He guessed that was because with the job he was doing, he was usually on his belly looking up at her. One night, she stopped right alongside him to get unloaded, and he got to his feet to get closer to her.

"I stroked her neck and said something to her, like 'Easy there, easy.' What a neat, strong animal she was," he recalled. "Her eyes were wild, you could tell she was scared. Oh, hell, we were all scared." He wanted to say something to soothe her, he explained, because he was convinced she would never make it through the night. The next day, everyone was asking what happened to Reckless, figuring she was dead. "I just didn't see how she could live through that. But she did," he said. "I remember someone saying, 'She's okay.' I was just amazed that she could do that much. She was trained but, just the same, it was unbelievable."

Those nights, she also moved dead and wounded back to safety, carrying them laid across her back. Some trips, she would bring up a load of ammunition and bring back a Marine. The Korean Service Corps, older South Korean men hired for non-combat work—the Marines called them Chiggee-Bears—moved most of the casualties, along with the Marines themselves. But they used Reckless when they could, and were glad of the help. "For us to carry those guys got pretty heavy at times," Nelmark admitted. "She was very disciplined, actually behaved better than some of the troops that handled the same detail." In daylight, working with the recoilless rifle squads, she moved their casualties off the ridge, as well.

——— 4 ———

On March 28, the recoilless rifles were again set up before sunrise, and Reckless was already building the supply of shells near the gun sites. The enemy continued to wield the greater power, and twice more pushed back against Marine attacks. The recoilless gunners took on new targets, shifting from Vegas to enemy assembly areas on nearby hills. In the early afternoon, with the tide turning, Easy Company, Second Battalion, Fifth Regiment, pushed through and finally secured Vegas, though a few Chinese stubbornly refused to yield the summit. Reckless worked through much of the day with the recoilless rifles, then came back that night to haul more ammunition for the mortars. She was unstoppable and the guys were grateful. Twice more, in the evening, the Chinese attacked Vegas, but this time the Marines forced them back. Carson, coming under fire at the same time, also held firm in Marine hands.

The days on the front line, fighting for the Nevada Cities, were midpoint in the two years Corporal Joe Stearns spent in Korea. It must have seemed a long time ago at that point but he, too, had dropped out of high school, his in South Milwaukee, Wisconsin, despite being a good student and athlete, to get to the war zone. Indeed, he volunteered to go ahead of a married guy with two kids. "John Wayne did a good job recruiting us," he admitted. "I was going to win the war, only I soon found out I wasn't able to do it." Mainly, though, he went in because he wanted to be a Marine, and he remained in the Corps for nine years, before heading for college and a career in teaching and school administration.

Stearns was part of Easy Company, Second Battalion, Fifth Regiment—"Easy does it," he laughed—but admitted that, over the years, he buried much of the awfulness they all encountered those five days of fighting. "By the second day of the battle, 56 percent of my company was wiped out," he said. As riflemen, Stearns and his squad were up front, ahead of everyone else. "What I know is, I was wounded the first day and wounded the last day. None of them were terrible wounds, and I kept going because I didn't want to desert my buddies," he said matter-of-factly. "It was horrible, carnage everywhere. I lost a lot of friends."

Like the others, he was totally unprepared to see Reckless, especially in the middle of a battlefield. "I didn't know a thing about her beforehand. 'Look at that,' I said. 'There's a damn horse.' I thought it was pretty neat. Everybody was admiring her." He added, "She saved a heck of a lot of human labor, and it saved lives. That was one heroic job, carrying that ammunition, constantly going back and forth."

The Chinese did not give up easily. In the early hours of March 29, they attacked again and were again repulsed. Just before 5:00 a.m., Easy Company and Fox Company, both Second Battalion, Fifth Regiment, made the final assault that effectively ended the battle and secured Outpost Vegas. With that, the Marines began rebuilding their installation. Yet, it didn't end there. That night, the Chinese again attacked, hitting Vegas from both sides. But aided by planes dropping flares that made the darkened battlefield appear as if in daylight, Marines struck back savagely and the enemy took heavy casualties.

Early the following morning, March 30, the Chinese took one more resounding shot at Vegas. Then they gave up. There was, however, one brief postscript—at about 11:00 a.m., a small and, as it turned out, suicidal event. Initially, the Marines thought the five approaching Chinese wanted to surrender, until they began hurling grenades and ripping the summit with machine gun fire. Suffering no casualties of their own, the Marines killed three of the attackers outright and took two prisoners, one of whom also died. No one knows who said it first, but a good ending line made the rounds. The enemy, sneered the Marines, had rolled the dice and they had come up snake eyes.

As for Reckless, by then she was back behind the front line, safe in her bunker, likely sound asleep. If she had stayed awake long enough, once again her buddies would have fed and watered her, and rubbed her down to soothe her muscles and help her relax. And if she had fallen asleep before they had a chance to fuss over her, they would have covered her with her blanket—a gentle gesture for a job very well done.

—— 5 ——

For the Marines caught in the five-day battle, March 1953 changed the common axiom about the month, that it came in like a lion and went out like a lamb. Had they thought about it, they would surely have said the lamb never showed up. March went out roaring.

The battle for Outpost Vegas ended officially on the morning of March 30. The gamble had been won. Although Reno was lost, Vegas and Carson stayed in U.N. hands. Outpost Elko came on line as a new, well-fortified installation, occupying the territory formerly known as Reno Block. Appropriately, it was named for another Nevada city.

Marine losses were the worst the Corps encountered in any battle of the Korean War. Chinese losses were far greater, plus the Marines had effectively put the 358th Chinese Regiment out of commission. According to a prisoner of war, the enemy's plan was to occupy Reno and Vegas, both of which overlooked enemy supply routes, before the expected U.N. spring offensive.

Incredibly, Reckless had survived a battle that took so many lives. "Some make it, some don't," said Wadley. "It's just dumb luck." Small as she was, she was a big target, but she came through. Any guy who saw her during that battle never forgot her. "It was that incredible spirit that she had. Those of us who were in that battle would have loved to have gotten out of there instantly, called it a peaceful day and gone home," Wadley continued. "But we knew we were there for the duration, either coming out on a stretcher or walking out after it was over. And she was right there with us until the end. Nobody cut her any slack.

"She was with that bunch of 75ers, with them the whole time, and she just melted in. It was all one unit. What they felt, she felt," Wadley explained, adding that the opposite would have also been true. "Sometimes horses are the most stabilizing thing in the middle of fear, which would have helped the guys. You think to yourself, 'If she isn't scared, why am I so scared?' It worked both ways.

"She was one of them, that was all there was to it. Hell, she could have run off, run all the way to Seoul for that matter. But no, she hung right in there. Just another Fifth Marine." The bond was the same as with anyone who was there. Wadley described it as a nod that said, "Yup, we know, we were there. She was with us."

A week later, the Fifth Regiment and their warhorse rotated back to reserve Camp Rose. Neither Harold Wadley nor Jack Nelmark ever saw Reckless after Vegas. Joe Stearns saw her in reserve, bearing treats when he visited. To each, her memory is indelible. Wadley still calls her the best horse he has ever known. Nelmark has told her story over and over, and people shake their heads in amazement. And Stearns talks to high school students each year about the Korean War, and they always ask to hear about Reckless.

Sharing a one-on-one with Sergeant Jack Railo. *(Courtesy Howard "Jack" Railo)*

Coached by Sergeant Joe Latham, Reckless steps over communication wires. *(Courtesy Leatherneck Magazine)*

Corporals John Gustafson (left) and Roland Bergstrom are among many who keep her company. *(Courtesy Roland Bergstrom)*

Waiting in her trailer as guys debate how to get the rig out of a ditch. *(Courtesy Roland Bergstrom)*

All bandaged up, she gets tons of attention for her barbed wire cut. *(Courtesy Quentin Seidel)*

Not shy about visiting, Reckless stops by Corporal Jerry Smigiel's tent. *(Courtesy Gerald Smigiel)*

Latham and Reckless, ready to climb to the front line. *(Courtesy Marine Corps)*

The recoilless rifle, for which she hauls shells. *(Courtesy Roland Bergstrom)*

With eyes closed, in Corporal Paul Hammersley's arms. *(Courtesy Paul Hammersley)*

She hops right into her little utility trailer.
(Courtesy Marine Corps Archives)

Coming back from the front line, Sergeant Pete Kitral often hitches a ride.
(Courtesy Julian "Pete" Kitral)

The first time at a gun site, Reckless rears at the blast, then moments later calmly munches grass.
(Courtesy Leatherneck Magazine)

In her bunker, she pokes her head out for a hug from Corporal Bergstrom.
(Courtesy Roland Bergstrom)

When needed, she hauls the whole recoilless rifle, barrel strapped to one side, tripod on the other.
(Courtesy Dept. of Defense, USMC, A171729)

Stringing communication wire, Reckless does the job of a dozen men in a day.
(Courtesy Leatherneck Magazine)

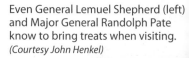

Even General Lemuel Shepherd (left) and Major General Randolph Pate know to bring treats when visiting. *(Courtesy John Henkel)*

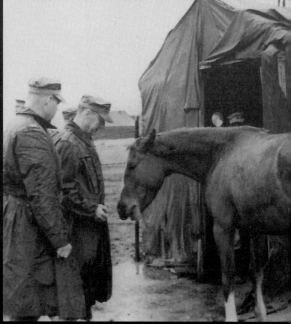

She wants to be right in the middle of whatever is going on. *(Courtesy John Henkel)*

Her handlers challenge the 1953 Kentucky Derby winner to a race against Reckless. *(Courtesy Leatherneck Magazine)*

A bareback spin with Corporal Hammersley.
(Courtesy Paul Hammersley)

Post Armistice she visits Camp Semper Fidelis, among other stops. *(Courtesy James Flannigan)*

Reckless' favorite.

With her buddies, Reckless is ready to party. *(Courtesy Leatherneck Magazine)*

At the front, Reckless is
promoted to sergeant
in a formal ceremony.
(Courtesy Michael Lavaia)

One of her most devoted
fans, General Pate pins
her chevrons on.
(Courtesy Marine Corps Archives)

Her buddies congratulate their newest officer. *(Courtesy Joseph Roy)*

A new sheet replaces the one she
shredded while enroute.
(Courtesy Leatherneck Magazine)

Sailing on the SS Pacific
Transport, her stall is on deck
behind the wheelhouse.
(Courtesy James Burneson)

Walking off the ship with
Lieutenant Eric Pedersen,
Reckless arrives in San Francisco.
(Courtesy Leatherneck Magazine)

She watches intently as Major General John Selden signs the Camp Pendleton guest book for her. *(Courtesy Marine Corps Archives)*

At the Marine Corps birthday banquet, Katherine Pedersen offers Reckless the first piece of cake. *(Courtesy Leatherneck Magazine)*

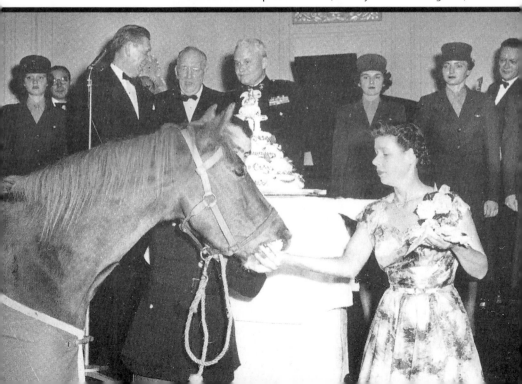

Proud mother with Fearless by her side. *(Courtesy Dept. of Defense, USMC, A367822)*

siting with his sons, Sergeant John Henkel
members Reckless' love of beer.
ourtesy John Henkel)

The winning name gets
Private First Class Robert E. Gibbs a
nose rub from Reckless' first born.
(Courtesy First Marine Division, USMC)

Mother and son, Dauntless, review the troops.
(Courtesy Marine Corps Archives)

Old friends, Reckless and General Pate, pose together after he promotes her to staff sergeant and Dauntless to private first class.
(Courtesy Marine Corps Archives)

Again doing the honors, General Pate pins on her insignia.
(Courtesy Dept. of Defense, USMC, A367953)

A postcard on sale at the Camp Pendleton Post Exchange. *(Courtesy Gerald Smigiel)*

As she is formally retired, Reckless watches Marines parade in her honor one last time, then exits with a huge whinny. *(Courtesy Marine Corps Archives)*

A statue of Staff Sergeant Reckless stands at the National Museum of the Marine Corps in Virginia. (*Courtesy National Museum of the Marine Corps*)

Chapter Five

WRAPPING UP THE WAR

—— 1 ——

U After 68 days on line, the Fifth Regiment packed up and headed south to reserve Camp Rose, hot showers, clean clothes, fresh cooked meals, and roomy tents with wooden floors. Leaving behind bunkers dug into the earth and four-man tents pitched on soggy hillsides, the men might have thought they were checking into a fine hotel. It was not the same as R&R, those few days of rest and recreation that some guys had the chance to enjoy in Tokyo. Just the same, with the men clear of incoming shells, everyone's adrenalin rushes could subside measurably.

Early in the Korean War, the U.N. command had established a number of reserve camps across the Korean Peninsula, large tracts of land several miles behind the MLR, that could accommodate as many as 5,000 men, with their weapons, supplies, motor vehicles, and everything else Marines brought back from the front line. Military units rotated in and out of the camps as their schedules dictated, usually taking up a portion of the grounds and having troops from other companies, battalions, regiments, services, or even other countries as neighbors.

Reserve camp might not have meant as much to Reckless when the Fifth Regiment rotated back to one in late December 1952, but it would this time.

Even when Sergeant Latham started pushing harder to get her ready for combat, even after the raids on Un-gok and Outpost Detroit, nothing remotely came close to what Reckless and her Marines had just been through in the Battle for the Nevada Cities. The guys said as much and, even if she did not have the words, Reckless knew it well. Like everyone else, she was beat and needed a rest. But tired and grungy as she was, this time Reckless picked up the vibes of some better days ahead.

The switch in regimental positions in April 1953—the Fifth Regiment to reserve, the First Regiment remaining on line, and the Seventh Regiment moving up to the front line was a typical rotation following the Marines' standard organizational formula of keeping two of any type of unit on line and one in reserve. Generally speaking, it meant two regiments were up front and one back in reserve; within each regiment, two battalions would be up and one back; and within each battalion, two companies would be up and one back. All of this, of course, was subject to change at any time, depending on what moves the enemy made—as a case in point, the battle for the Nevada Cities.

For the guys in reserve, beyond the amenities of room and board—not the least of which meant swapping clothes they had worn much too long for freshly laundered attire—the fallback position meant two things: training and more training, to stay sharp for the next round of fighting, and maintaining the Marines' secondary line of defense, in the event that the MLR was overrun by the Chinese. That month, the fallback position, known as the Kansas Line, having taken a beating from the spring thaw and heavy rains, was ready for considerable repairs.

There was a hopeful sign in Panmunjom, the first in six months. At the height of the fighting over the Nevada Cities, the Communists had sent word to Army General Mark Clark, commander of the U.N. forces, that they were interested in resuming peace talks. Specifically, they would allow the exchange of sick and wounded prisoners of war, dubbed Little Switch, to go forward. Beyond that, they were willing to reopen truce negotiations. As a show of good faith on both sides, Little Switch was accomplished quickly, with all involved repatriated to their home countries in seven days beginning April 20, 1953. That done, the two sides resumed talks a week later, on April 26.

This time, the pressure was on to stay at the table, the result of some clear changes in the political landscape. For one, the new U.S. President, Dwight D. Eisenhower, raised concerns among the opposition as to how he wanted to end the Korean conflict. As a former five-star general, and a member of the Republican Party, in which there were some decidedly hawkish elements, the North Koreans wondered if Eisenhower hoped to end the war by winning it? Then in March, Soviet Premier Joseph Stalin died, taking from North Korea a major patron. Internally, the struggle for who would succeed Stalin turned other Soviet leaders away from any potentially disruptive situations, in this case an escalation of the Korean War. Indeed, all of the proxy powers—the U.S. and its U.N. colleagues, the Soviet Union, and Communist China—all recognized that the toll of the conflict had become too great, both financially and in human costs, and each wanted out.

Opinion polls taken in the spring of 1953 indicated that the American public, by a wide margin never in favor of the Korean War, now strongly supported ending the fighting. The caveat was that watching the peace talks drag on for more than a year had sapped confidence that an agreement could be reached. The fate of sick and injured prisoners had been resolved, but what would become of the more than 85,000 other prisoners of war (POWs), most of who were troops from the north? Not surprisingly, the enemy wanted all POWs still held by the U.N.

Command returned to North Korea or Communist China, no matter what the individual wished. Equally unsurprising, many of these U.N. prisoners wanted to go to South Korea or Taiwan, rather than return to their home countries. Mindful of what happened at the end of World War II, when POWs were forced to return to their home countries, including many to the Soviet Union, the U.S. was insistent that prisoners of the Korean War must be free to choose where they would go. Negotiations were protracted but, in the end, the POWs were given that choice.

South Korean President Syngman Rhee was unequivocally against any arrangements that did not unify the Koreas under his country. When his list of demands were discouraged—first the prospect of unification, then the size of his postwar military support from the United States—Rhee jarred the peace talks by releasing 25,000 North Korean and Communist Chinese POWs housed in several jails across South Korea. The mass exodus, Rhee insisted, was a prison break. Indicative, perhaps, of the muscle now behind the talks in these final few months, negotiations were rocked but did not break off. Indeed, in a curious twist, the dispersal of so many prisoners was face-saving for the North Koreans. Their return was out of North Korea's control, and spared them the embarrassment of acknowledging that many of their captured troops did not want to come home.

------- 2 -------

Through April, with the Fifth Regiment temporarily settled at Camp Rose, about a mile north of the Imjin River, Marines were kept busy with a full training schedule of field exercises and lectures. For the time being, activity at the front had quieted down, but no one trusted that to last. The enemy had lain low before and reappeared, and the expectation was that it would do it again. Reserve troops had to stay combat ready, in the event that any part of the regiment was directed to move back to the front.

On April 13, the Second Battalion and other units of the Fifth Regiment were ordered to begin an amphibious maneuver, known as MARLEX, for Marine Landing Exercise. Boarding transport ships at Inchon harbor, about 30 miles west of Seoul, the troops would proceed to Tokchok-to, one of the offshore islands south of Inchon where they would hit the beaches.

As was required, the Marines filed a manifest with the Navy, a detailed list of what they would bring aboard for use in the upcoming exercise. This time, however, two unusual items jumped from the page: one horse with two days' rations. Dismissing them as bogus, the Navy assumed that the Marines were trying to pull a fast one and smuggle something on board—liquor, perhaps, or pokey bait, slang for candy. Indeed, it was a moment of disbelief when Reckless arrived, shipping helmet on and carrying four recoilless rifle shells strapped to her packsaddle. The Captain, who proudly skippered a ship that had won an award for cleanliness two years in a row, was not amused.

High winds and rough seas caused the maneuvers to be curtailed, but not before the Marines made their island landing, nor before Reckless had decided this activity was not to her liking. A makeshift stall had been set up for her in the hold of the ship, and because of the stormy weather, she did not go ashore as planned, but was left on board while her buddies hit the beaches. While horses do not get seasick, it is possible that she became agitated at being left alone in strange surroundings. Stomping around her stall, and tracking her bedding into a pile of muck, as well as losing her appetite, could well have been the result.

According to the Regiment's command diary, the maneuver was

shortened to four days, and the Marines were back at Inchon on April 17. Undoubtedly relieved to see her buddies on board for the return trip to the mainland, Reckless regained her appetite and, according to earlier versions of the story, polished off the rations brought for her. Out of food, her Marines claimed she nevertheless wanted nothing to do with what the ship's galley had to offer. And whatever it was, the cooks likely were annoyed at having to dish up anything at all. Displeasure on both sides mounted. Apparently, against Navy wishes, the Marines took matters into their own hands and had a cutter resupply the ship with food she would eat.

The Marines remembered Reckless' voyage with amusement, but not their Navy hosts, who took a dim view of the Fifth Regiment and their beloved warhorse. As they left the ship, not one Marine recalled any Navy personnel saying so much as, "Come again." Years later, Joe Latham still laughed, "Every one of those guys like to have gone haywire."

----- **3** -----

Thirteen months after they had assumed defense of the Western Sector, on May 5, 1953, the First Marine Division officially left the front line, its position taken over by the U.S. Army 25th Division and the attached Turkish Brigade. The Marines went into I Corps Reserve—I Corps designating the combined U.S. Army/U.S. Marines fighting force, a military organization particular to the Korean War. For four days before the change of duties, well over 2,000 truckloads of personnel and equipment relocated the entire Marine division to Camp Casey, south of the Imjin River and about 40 miles north of Seoul.

By this time in the war, the huge complex had hosted a variety of military units, of not only U.S. troops but also other U.N. participants. Among them were the Royal Thai Battalion, the 19th Battalion Combat Team of the Philippines, the U.S. Army 45th

Division, the First and Second Australian Regiments, as well as, now, the Marine First Division. Spread over the camp's three sections, the Seventh Regiment and the First Korean Marine Corps Regiment were housed in Camp Indianhead, to the north; the First Regiment was housed in Camp Britannia, to the south; and the Fifth Regiment and the Division Command Post were housed in Camp Casey itself.

In the midst of trucks rolling back and forth to accomplish the massive move, somebody in the Recoilless Rifle Platoon must have realized that on Saturday, May 2, 1953—the first Saturday in May—at Churchill Downs, in Louisville, Kentucky, the Kentucky Derby was being run. Did some of the guys stop whatever they were doing to listen to Armed Forces Radio, sing along with the playing of "My Old Kentucky Home," and hear the call of the race? That part is speculation, but the plan that was hatched thereafter was real enough to hit the newspapers. Reckless, the aspiring racehorse before her life took a different turn, should have a race—and her buddies were ready to issue a challenge.

The Run for the Roses was an upset, Dark Star, a 25-to-1 long shot, narrowly beating the favorite, Native Dancer. With that, Sergeant Latham, through Marine Corps Headquarters in Washington, D.C., invited newspaper publisher and philanthropist, Harry Guggenheim, to send his champion three-year-old to South Korea. The offer was a handicap race against Reckless, each entrant to carry weight in the form of recoilless rifle shells. Why Guggenheim did not respond is unknown, but perhaps he and his champion thoroughbred were caught up in the post-race excitement in Kentucky. Undeterred, Reckless and her Marines bided their time until Native Dancer regained his form and won the Preakness Stakes, the second leg of the Triple Crown, two weeks later at Pimlico Racetrack in Maryland.

This time, the challenge was to Alfred Vanderbilt II, a

prominent force behind Thoroughbred racing in the U.S., to send Native Dancer, the conditions to be the same as were set down for Dark Star. The Pacific edition of the *Stars and Stripes* picked up the story, running the headline, "Marine Mare Dares Dancer." And in St. Petersburg, Florida, Joe Latham's hometown, the newspaper dubbed Reckless "A Korean Speedster" over the banner head, "Mare of the Mad Marines Challenges Native Dancer." According to her handlers, by then Reckless had an impressive racing record as winner of the Paddy Derby at Outpost Vegas, and as the unchallenged titleholder of Korea's Upsan Downs. But alas, Vanderbilt also silently dodged the opportunity to place Native Dancer in Reckless' fast company. No one was surprised, of course, but everyone had a good laugh.

Reserve camp was easy on Reckless. When she was called upon to work, she was sharp and ready to go, whether accompanying one of the recoilless rifle squads when its firepower was needed, or rolling out communication wire—comwire, the guys called it—a never-ending requirement in camp. The rest of the time she was at liberty, grazing on scrub grass where she could find it, and hanging out with her buddies. Busy as they were, in reserve there was more time to give to Reckless, and many more visitors. Guys who remembered her during the fight for Outpost Vegas came by, as did others who had only heard about the work she had done. Reserve camps had perimeter fences, so even if they fenced off a paddock and built Reckless a shed, she wasn't in it most of the time. She stayed where there was activity, and as one of the guys put it, "She was going to sleep in somebody's tent if she wanted, anyway."

One night, perhaps looking for a place to settle down, Reckless happened upon a poker game in full swing. Latham was at the table, a pile of chips growing in front of him. She stood behind him, silently watching the way the chips caught the light as Latham moved them about. Her lunge was smooth, surprising everyone as she thrust her head in and scooped up a mouthful of the chips. Latham was on his feet and had his hand in her mouth almost as fast, retrieving what he could. But years later, though with great good humor, he still insisted she ate him out of 30 bucks.

It was also in reserve camp that she crossed paths with Corporal Wally Stewart. Reckless and her entourage were strutting their stuff, swaggering down one of the main roadways. They seemed to be moving as one piece, little Reckless in the center with two or three Marines on either side, arms linked, laughing and kicking up dust. It was just too perfect, remembered Stewart. He and some of his cohorts from Baker Company, First Battalion, First Regiment, were to the side of the road, just itching for the others to get closer. As Stewart explained, "Marines being what they are, they are going to needle you at any chance. Oh, hell, the first thing I yelled was, 'What's that stupid horse doing here?'" And then everyone piled on, each side giving as good as it got. Stewart, of course, remembered Baker's side the best.

"Hey, what do we have here?"

"Looks like a funny looking dog to me."

"I'd say the Pogey Bait Fifth have themselves a horse."

"How can you tell? They all look like horses asses to me."

Insulting Reckless was bad enough, but calling the Fighting Fifth, as the Fifth Regiment is known, pogey bait—suggestive of something sweet and soft—was even worse. Then Pisstube entered the fray. Baker Company's little Korean mutt had been saved from some mommasan's stew pot, and was named for a key feature of front line urinals, the erect pipes that were stuck every few feet in gravel-filled troughs. He was a feisty little guy, and when the company was on line, would start growling if Chinese were in the area, picking up the scent sooner than the Marines did.

His buddies believed that Pisstube did not like horses, and would certainly want to fight with one owned by the Fifth Marines. Reckless was a few steps past, when they let him run after her, barking and trying to nip her heels. Unfortunately, no one warned the dog that horses, with their 180-degree vision, can aim a hind kick with precision. Reckless let fly with a few warning shots, and Pisstube took the hint. No one was hurt.

For Reckless' part, it laid to rest talk about her being afraid of dogs. Joe Gordon, her buddy from Hawaii, knew it was nonsense. She had bonded with his two dogs, Blackie and Brownie early on, the three of them sometimes laying down together in the sun on the parade grounds. He couldn't help but be amused.

It was the only time Wally Stewart saw Reckless in Korea, but the attachment remained. "She was a fabulous horse, and she did well for those guys," he said. "There are probably a lot of them around today that wouldn't be here if it wasn't for her. It was an amazing relationship." In the fall of 1953, Stewart returned to San Francisco, California and, after a couple of false starts, got serious about an education. He eventually became a high school math teacher and was always fond of saying that his students never did anything that "he hadn't seen or done himself." Through the years, when he would visit Camp Pendleton, he always stopped to see Reckless.

4

Reckless was losing friends, Marines who had been in Korea 12 months or more and were heading stateside. Lieutenant Pedersen was among them, reluctant though he was to leave his men and their horse. It was the pattern in the Korean War, individuals within a unit rotated out and others came in, sometimes one at a time, or in twos, or threes. Different from some other wars, when an entire unit replaced another, in Korea the faces changed over a year's time but the unit itself remained. Eventually, Reckless had a whole new set of friends, guys who came to know her later in the war and bonded with her just as the old friends had.

Paul Hammersley, a 21-year-old from Bargersville, Indiana, arrived in Korea in the spring of 1953, happy to find himself assigned to Headquarters Company, Fifth Regiment. Informed during the voyage over that he was going to be a 0-300, he countered, "Sergeant, there's got to be a mistake. That's a basic rifleman." The reply was a brusque, "Boy, the Marine Corps don't make no mistakes."

Somehow, though, there was a change, and Corporal Hammersley spent almost his entire 12-month tour at Headquarters Company. It was where Reckless spent most of her time, and in short order, she had a new friend. As it turned out, he was one she could count on for the brew in the light golden can that she had grown fond of. One Sunday afternoon, Hammersley lay down for a nap, tired from walking guard duty most of the previous night. His monthly ration of two cases of Goebel beer was stashed under his cot.

Reckless, savvy about where things were, came into Hammersley's tent. "I was sound asleep," he recalled, "and I felt this terrible pain. She was biting my arm to wake me up." Though startled, he knew right away what she wanted, and opened a beer for her. Lapping it up from a pan, she accepted a second beer from another guy, then polished off peanut butter and jelly sandwiches brought from the mess hall.

"She just made everybody happy," Hammersley said. "She'd trot up to you, and you'd pet her a little bit, then go on your way. She took your mind off everything else."

Sometimes at night, she would fall in and walk the perimeter with whoever was on guard duty, staying with them a while, then moving off. "It was pretty good having a horse with you. She could hear better and smell better," Hammersley admitted. "For that short amount of time she was there, I felt just a little bit safer. It was a comfort to have her with you."

By the spring of 1953, Reckless had put on weight and shed out her heavy winter coat. Connected as she was with her buddies, more and more it seemed like everyone pitched in to care for her. Corporal Quentin Seidel, self-described as the designated farm boy from Nebraska, was a couple of years out of high school when, as he put it, "I got it in my head to join the Marine Corps." In Korea, assigned to the Fifth Regiment, Anti-Tank Company, he volunteered as a company driver. Usually, it was his job to take Reckless to Seoul when she needed new shoes. Indeed, keeping Reckless' feet trimmed and shod was of ongoing importance, especially given the beating they took on the rough Korean terrain.

This particular trip, Hammersley got the nod to go along. It was routine enough, albeit a long day—the small utility trailer, the slow drive over dusty roads, all reminiscent of Reckless' first trip to reserve camp so many months ago. But this day was not going to go as well. Her friends knew that Reckless had a strong personality—sweet and loving, to be sure, but definite about what she wanted, and insistent if need be. When Seidel and Hammersley found a farrier, near the old Seoul racetrack, she made very clear that she wanted nothing to do with him.

Neither had ever seen her behave like she did, baring her teeth, pinning her ears, rolling her eyes, and acting for all the world as if she was ready to bite or kick the farrier. The Korean was terrified. "All we had ever seen was the gentle side of her," explained Hammersley. "We knew this was not going to work." Afraid for the farrier's safety, they got Reckless back in her trailer and away from his establishment as quickly as they could.

Her mood was not much improved at meeting the next farrier they found, but the two Marines prevailed upon her to calm down and relax, and the shoeing went forward. He used the hot shoeing method, a process in which the metal plate is heated in a forge until it is red hot, then laid briefly against the bottom surface of the bare hoof wall. Startling as it looks to the uninitiated, it does not hurt the horse. The scorch marks on the hoof are where the farrier files the bottom edge so that it fits tightly with the shoe which, once cooled in water, is nailed on. The work was expertly done, and farrier and client got along quite well, Hammersley recalled. Reckless left happy in her new shoes.

With that, the three headed to camp, the Marines showing proper documents at Freedom Bridge, so that no one would think they were stealing a horse. It had been a perplexing day. Did something about the first farrier remind Reckless of a previous unpleasant experience? Perhaps some old-timer had handled her in a rougher, less humane way as they did in the past, restraining her with ropes to keep her from moving while being shod? The Marines would never know, nor was there ever another unnerving story about getting Reckless shod. Suffice to say, she was not shy about her likes, or what she would have nothing whatsoever to do with, this little pony with the big personality.

——— 5 ———

Despite hopes that progress toward a peace agreement would slow the pace of the war, the Chinese again ratcheted up the fight. Following the battles for Outposts Carson, Reno, and Vegas, there had been a lull until, at the end of May, the enemy turned its sights back to the Nevada Cities. Under heavy enemy pressure, the Army, then in control of the Carson-Elko-Vegas complex, withdrew its forces. Two months after the Marines had held Carson and Vegas, and increased the defenses on the new installation, Outpost Elko, the capture of the outposts by the Chinese left the MLR more vulnerable than it had previously been.

In late June 1953, the First Marine Division came back on line, relieving the Army's 25th Infantry Division. A new Division Commander, Major General Randolph McCall Pate, replaced Major General Edwin A. Pollack. Moving from the Camp Casey complex to the front were the Fifth Regiment, to hold the western portion of the Marine Sector, and the Seventh Regiment, to hold the eastern portion. The First Regiment remained in regimental reserve. Upon meeting Reckless, General Pate was captivated by her, and the relationship between her and the other Marines, and he would remain her devoted fan for the rest of his life.

The Korean War grew bloodier in June and July 1953. In some of the worst fighting of the conflict, the Communists lost an estimated 100,000 men, while gaining a few miles of hilly-to-mountainous real estate. U.N. casualties, at about half that number, were still a terrible price to pay. On July 8, as the First Marine Division formerly assumed operational control of the Western Sector, the Seventh Regiment's hold on Outposts Berlin and East Berlin was severely challenged. The loss of Outpost Vegas in May, had put the Berlins in greater jeopardy, and on July 19 they, too, fell to the Chinese. The Seventh Marines held Boulder City but the cascading affect, with the two Berlins gone, made it more vulnerable.

By mid-July, the Fifth Regiment was again tangling with the Chinese. In the move that brought the First Marine Division back to the front line, the Fifth Regiment had returned to familiar territory, again establishing their camp east of the town of Changdan. It was the first forward camp that Reckless had known, when the Marines moved up on line the previous October. The area had natural boundaries with hills surrounding a valley floor, and one road for both access and exit. In October, Reckless had wandered away, creating worry and fear among her Marines. But this time Reckless knew where she belonged, and there were no instances of her disappearing.

An armistice agreement was in place on July 20, yet the enemy fought on. Fifth Marines holding Outposts Esther, Hedy, Dagmar, and Ingrid, had already withstood attacks in the previous few days, thanks to artillery support from the 11th Regiment. The Fifth's Second Battalion continued to patrol from Outpost Ava, some four miles east of the Peace Corridor, to Combat Outpost 2, a couple of miles up from the MLR and a half mile from the edge of the Corridor. Reckless was on call, whenever an enemy hot spot needed to be dealt with by the recoilless rifles.

Not only were the Chinese attacking above ground, but it became clear that they were tunneling toward COP2. In a fire mission virtually identical to the one in October 1952, during which the Marines leveled the North Korean hamlet of Kamon-dong, once again a recoilless rifle squad was ordered to set up just inside the right angle, where the Peace Corridor intersected the Circle. From there, the Marines proceeded to give the enemy a good shellacking without the risk of return fire, some of which would likely land in the No Fire Zone, a few yards behind the fire squad. Unlike the previous fall, when the newly arrived Reckless had yet to be trained and outfitted for her job, for this assignment she was saddled up and ready to haul shells.

With three days left until the Armistice was to be signed and take effect, the Chinese struck again. Just before midnight on July 24, Fifth Marines on Outposts Dagmar and Esther were again attacked, again without success. With first light on July 26, the last of the fighting subsided. The tally was East Berlin and Berlin to the enemy; Boulder

City, Dagmar, and Esther remaining in Marine hands. However, First Division casualties for the last month of the Korean War were high, in all 1,611. Of some consolation, enemy casualties were thought to be double that or more.

At 10:00 a.m. on Monday, July 27, 1953, in a stark ceremony at Panmunjom, the Armistice to end the fighting was signed by U.S. Army Lieutenant General William Harrison Jr., representing the United Nations Command, and General Nam II, representing the North Korean People's Army and the Chinese People's Volunteer Army. The cease-fire called for both sides to withdraw 2,000 yards behind their front lines, in effect creating the Demilitarized Zone. The following morning, they were to reclaim the bodies of those killed in recent days; and in the next three days, remove all equipment and supplies, mark the existence of mines and other hazards, and begin cleaning up the area.

Twelve hours after the signing, at 10:00 p.m., the front line fell silent and the Korean War was over. In his exceptional wartime chronicle, *The Last Parallel*, Martin Russ remembered how the night sky lighted up in a pyrotechnic display of white star clusters, and red and yellow flares, all along the 150-mile front from the Yellow Sea to the Sea of Japan, signifying the end of a battle that had no winners. "Men appeared along the trench, some of them had shed their helmets and flak jackets," he wrote. The Chinese were singing, and then, "A hundred yards or so down the trench, someone began shouting the Marine Corps Hymn at the top of his lungs. Others joined in, bellowing the words." In different keys, and phrases apart, everyone was singing:

From the halls of Montezuma
To the shores of Tripoli;
We will fight our country's battles

In the air, on land and sea;
First to fight for right and freedom
And to keep our honor clean;
We are proud to claim the title
Of United States Marine.

And Russ added, as if underscoring the reality, "We all smoked for the first time in the MLR trench."

Three years, one month, and two days after it had begun, the so-called police action was over. Active fighting had stopped, though nobody was sure if the peace would hold. The troops were skeptical, watchful, and waiting. Still, on the night of July 27, wherever in camp her buddies were celebrating, Reckless would have been right there, enjoying the moment. Someone would have poured her a Goebel or two, and probably fixed up a couple of peanut butter and jelly sandwiches to go along with them.

Chapter Six

SERGEANT RECKLESS, MA'AM

————— 1 —————

U In the broiling heat of those summer months in 1953, with temperatures reaching into the 90s, the Marines dismantled their sector of the front line and hauled the debris away. Filling in trenches, bulldozing tank slots, and salvaging timber from bunkers crushed back into hillsides, the defense line of a war just ended was itself destroyed. The sounds of battle had ceased, but in their place, sounds of demolition and reconstruction signaled a continuing state of combat readiness. As many guys said, the quiet was suspect, and the suspicion was that sooner or later the enemy would break the cease-fire.

Three days was what each side had, from the time the Armistice was signed, to move all troops and equipment back from the MLR. In the Western Sector, thousands of U.S. and South Korean Marines worked around the clock to tear apart outposts and main line fortifications. Whatever heavy machinery they could put in play, they did—along with bulldozers, tow trucks, other trucks with power winches, even helicopters to short-hop timber to collection depots. Beyond that, it was sheer manpower—to hoist timber from rubble to truck beds, or to grappling chains for airlifts, to pack up and load equipment, and the rest.

Not surprisingly, torrential rains appeared like clockwork that summer as in years past, slowing and complicating the massive clean-up, which involved work details from every regimental company, and stretched another 45 days into mid-September. By then, the Fifth Regiment alone had hauled away 12 tons of equipment and supplies. Much of it was recyclable, and as quickly as it was torn down found its way into new construction at the regiment's new position. With the pull back still north of the Imjin River, the transfer of all that materiel was swift and uncomplicated, and the Fifth was resettled the fastest of any military units. Now known as the Northern Regiment, the Fifth's post-combat assignment was to secure and police that part of the newly created Demilitarized Zone (the DMZ) within the First Marine Division sector.

Reckless did not help with the demolition. She was on break, but like every other Marine, she was ready in case the enemy broke the cease-fire agreement and they were called back to the front. In the meantime, she was hanging out and roaming the compound at will. Along with eating, it was her other favorite past time—and probably how she got her ear split, thought Corporal Quentin Seidel, who figured she poked her head through some concertina barbed wire and jerked it out too quickly. Sewing up farm animals was something he had done plenty of, and as soon as he saw what happened, he headed for the first aid station to get a needle and thread.

When Seidel added sulfa powder to his list of requests, so that he could disinfect the wound, the medic hit the ceiling. "I'm a ... I'm a people doctor, not an animal doctor," he sputtered. Then quickly realizing the unwelcome repercussions should he not help the regiment's warhorse, the Navy corpsman filled the request, handing Seidel a bottle half full of Sulfa pills, which he could mash, plus the requisite needle and thread.

Returning to where Reckless was waiting, he found a group of her buddies had gathered around her, ready to help out.

Laying her on her side, one of the guys held her head while Seidel sewed up the ear, sprinkled it with the Sulfa, and covered it in gauze. "I wrapped it up real good," he laughed. "She wandered around getting all kinds of sympathy for a long time, until I had to take the bandages off." Maybe she was even a little sorry when they came off, he had to wonder.

"She was just as calm as could be," Seidel recalled of his star patient. "She'd been with those guys so close and so much, she knew she wasn't going to really get hurt." And fixing her up, he added, "was something for everyone to do. She was just like one of the people around there."

With the cease-fire in place, the Marines watched and waited. The atmosphere was quiet but tense just the same, troops on both sides peering at each other through binoculars from a distance, or a whole lot closer. Sometimes, it was like eyeball-to-eyeball, said one. With defenses reconfigured, the Fifth Regiment pulled the toughest assignment, holding the most vulnerable portion of the new battle line. The frontage, some 36,000 yards (almost 20.5 miles) was about three times the territory usually occupied by the regiment while the war was ongoing. The boundaries now were to the north and west, the southern edge of the DMZ; to the east, the Samichon River; and to the south, the Imjin River, forded by two bridges in the Marine Sector, Freedom Gate and Spoonbill. With the division's supply center at Munsan-ni, it meant Fifth Marines crossed the river whenever they needed to restock anything.

The Marines' new forward defense line, installed as fast as the old one was torn down, was called the Outpost Line of Resistance (OPLR). Much the same as with the defunct MLR, this line was buffered by a number of outposts that served as observation points, as well as a first line of defense for the rest of the division. But how they were set up changed.

With overall troop strength declining, the new outposts were occupied by considerably fewer Marines, but were well fortified with automatic weapons and firepower.

——— **2** ———

Ten days after the Armistice was signed, Operation Big Switch commenced the process of repatriating the remaining 88,596 prisoners of war to their homelands, if they so chose. Involving ten times the number repatriated during Little Switch, it took until September 6 to complete. At 75,823, the overwhelming majority were North Koreans or Chinese. South Korean POWs accounted for another 7,862; all U.N. coalition forces, accounted for 4,911. Of the latter figure, 3,597 were Americans, including 197 Marines.

A major sticking point in the peace talks had been how the POWs would be dispersed. The U.S. was insistent that they not be forced to go home against their wishes, while North Korea and China opposed such self-determination. The solution called for the 22,000 POWs who refused repatriation to be held in a camp within the DMZ for an additional 90 days, during which time governments could attempt to persuade their countrymen to reconsider their choices. In the end, virtually all in this last group of POWs still wished to be relocated. Most were from North Korea or China, and chose instead to go to Taiwan or South Korea. A much smaller number—one British, 21 Americans, and 327 South Koreans—also refused to return to their home countries.

For the benefit of press and dignitaries, the Marines maintained a giant vertical map affixed to an outdoor pole at Munsan-ni for the duration of Operation Big Switch. As POWs were processed at Panmunjom, a Marine atop a ladder marked the southward progress of road convoys heading for Freedom Gate Bridge and their final destination on the other side, Freedom Village. Corporal Blaine Myers, with Fox Company, Second Battalion, Fifth Regiment, was stationed on the north side of the Imjin River, near the bridge, still manning a 60mm mortar. Once the prisoner switch was complete, Fox Company rotated back to reserve below the Imjin River, and this time it was Myers' turn to meet Reckless.

"When you got back to reserve, it was all spit shine and polish again," he pointed out, and on one particular day that meant a parade for a visiting Inspector General, followed by an inspection. An important visitor no matter what, it turned out that this one was a full Colonel or, as the guys would say, a Bird Colonel. "That's when I really got introduced to Reckless, because being from Tucson, Arizona, they figured I was a cowboy. So I got to hold her," he chuckled. In reality, it was not unknown territory. Myers had been raised around horses, and competed in riding events from the age of 12.

Passing in review, holding her by a lead, Reckless behaved beautifully, and when she stood for inspection, it was the same. "Everyone had an M1 except me. I had Reckless," he continued. As the Inspector General moved along the line, he opened the bolt on this rifle and that. Then he stopped in front of Myers.

"You a cowboy?" he said.

"I am today, sir," Myers replied.

The Colonel pursued the inquiry, asking if the Marine was taking good care of Reckless. "Yes, sir" came the answer, embellished in the retelling by, "I was holding on to her, anyway."

It could have ended there, except that almost as soon as the formation was dismissed, the PX truck rolled up. A mobile version of the Military Post Exchange, selling snacks, toiletries, film, and other whatnots, it only showed up twice a month, and Myers was not going to miss out. With Reckless in tow, he got in line and made his purchases.

"Right away she grabbed the package of cupcakes I'd bought, so that cost me," he said, remembering how fast she devoured them, cellophane and all. Trying again, he bought cookies, which he held close, while trying to keep his charge at arm's length. "She kept bumping me with her head, and trying to step on me. She wanted those cookies." Myers turned her loose, but by the time he did, it made no difference. "The faster I'd go, the fast she'd come at me. I'd try to get away, and she'd bite at me."

Running up the couple of steps to his tent, set on a hillside, he almost made it through the door when Reckless lunged one last time. "She grabbed me, my jacket, and the cookies," he said, admitting that it was all to the amusement of his buddies. Everyone laughed and no one helped. Pissed off at the time, he thought about taking a swing at her, but figured that if he got caught, he would have wound up in the brig. Reckless, however, decided she had a new friend, and every time thereafter when she saw Myers, she would come up to him, maybe to see what he had for her.

Calling her a typical Marine, Myers shrugged off the PX incident as one of her "off" moments, "because by the same token, we knew our place when we were in formation, and we were ready for combat all the time," he said. "And she was like that. She gave everything she had. She was all Marine, and she had our respect for that."

--- 3 ---

The Armistice called for both sides to withdraw 2,000 yards from the most forward position each held at the time of the cease-fire. Between them, the vacated territory, roughly two and a half miles wide, became the DMZ, and the line running through its center, the Military Line of Demarcation, was the dividing line between North and South Korea. To maintain the purpose of the DMZ, which was to function as a buffer between the two nations, each side was required to create a 1,000-man police force to maintain peace in their sector, a job accepted by the military. In the Marine Sector, it involved the creation of the 100-man First Provisional Demilitarized Zone Police Company, made up of 25 enlisted men and one officer from each regiment.

In September 1953, Corporal Jim Flannigan was one of the first Marines to join the force. Arriving in Korea the previous April, the Minnesota native was a machine gunner, then a radioman with Fox Company, Second Battalion, First Regiment, before taking the new position. "Selected" was the word used, Flannigan noted, in tapping individuals for the important assignment, and the Marines were equally pointed in describing what was expected of those chosen. "We were told, adamantly, that if we were caught on the other side of the demarcation line, there would be no help for us, and we could, in fact, start the Korean War all over again by breaking the truce. For me, an 18-year-old, that was enough warning to behave myself out there," he remembered, adding that he liked the adventurous edge of it all.

Meeting up with Reckless one day at Camp Semper Fidelis—or, as was usually said, Camp Semper Fi—was one of the lighter moments. Indeed, had Flannigan not had a camera on hand, her presence would have all but been forgotten. Yet, there she was, posing with members of the Provisional DMZ Police, wearing the new blanket that some of her buddies had chipped in to have sewn by a tailor in Seoul. Made of heavy scarlet silk with gold binding, in the official Marine Corps colors, it included the Corps' eagle, globe and anchor emblem on each side, surrounded by the wording, "5th Marines, AT Co, First Marine Division." Against the grays and greens of camp, Reckless in her blanket was the focal point of Flannigan's color photos.

"She had quite a reputation over there," he said. "She made the rounds." The appearances were scheduled, because they had advance notice that she would visit Camp Semper Fi, and after she left there, she went on to another unit. Presumably, commanding officers requested her presence, and Flannigan thought many across the Marine Sector did just that. "Reckless was a celebrity. It didn't take much to amuse combat weary Marines. She was certainly a welcome visitor to our unit."

The First Marine Division would stay in South Korea almost 20 months after the signing of the Korean War Armistice, during which time they contributed to the rebuilding of a war-torn country through the Armed Forces Assistance to Korea program (AFAK). A highly successful, mutual assistance endeavor, it functioned at the community level, utilizing local labor and materials from South Korea, and funds from there and the United States. U.S. servicemen provided technical assistance for an array of projects, the most wanted being schools, followed by orphanages, paved highways, civic buildings, hospitals, bridges, churches, and more. Marines undertook 51 projects, 42 of which were schools.

For those who got involved, their work not only helped to rebuild a shattered country, but it kept their mind off the waiting game. Most Marines were of the opinion that the enemy was planning another attack. It was just a matter of time, they thought, before they would be fighting again. Like a game of chess, each side watched the other closely and reacted when the other made a move, as Corporal Mike Mason remembered it. From Maryland, he arrived in Korea in November 1953, in time to experience "the coldest place I've ever known." He spent that first winter on an outpost north of the Imjin River near Freedom Gate Bridge, watching the POW camp in the DMZ. The several guys on the outpost were from the Fifth Regiment Recoilless Rifle Platoon but, after a crash course, Mason was manning a 90mm canon. In spring, they pulled the squad back to reserve, and he, an ace ping-pong player, met Sammy, the young Korean boy who beat him every game.

By then, Sammy was taking care of Reckless. Joe Latham had rotated home the previous October, and most of the others from her original circle had also gone. She obviously had adapted well to the change, though, because Mason's memory was that "she ran the compound." Like other reserve camps, it had a perimeter fence of barbed wire, not to keep the guys in but to keep the locals out. Still, they were apparently more conscientious about keeping her in her own shed with its paddock at night. Guards with live ammunition still patrolled the compound and, roaming loose in the dark, she could have been shot by mistake. Taking no chances that she could get out or be stolen, a Marine also stood guard outside her enclosure.

Days, however, Reckless was at liberty. "Any time we were sitting around, having a beer or whatever, she'd come nosing around," Mason recalled. Her love of Goebel beer continued unabated, and the guys obliged with a can or two. Then they would shoo her away, though always good-naturedly. One evening, just before mess, they sent her on her way, only to hear a huge ruckus a few minutes later. Mason could hear the cooks yelling, swearing up a storm. Cherry pie was on the menu that night, and around the corner of the mess tent, the big, two-feet by three-feet rectangles of pie had been set on a ledge to cool. They were still there, but now the center of each pie was gone, and so was the culprit. That night, cherry pie was off the menu. "We figured out in a hurry how to keep her from getting at any more of those pies," he laughed.

———— **4** ————

Though in smaller numbers now, replacements for the guys heading home kept showing up. Mike Lavaia, from Yonkers, New York, was among them in early 1954. After his dad, a World War I veteran, died, Lavaia was raised by his mother and grandfather, the latter a shoemaker who made tack for the horsemen at Yonkers Raceway. Lavaia had been out of high school for a couple of years, and was working for the Herald Statesman newspaper, when a friend suggested they join the Marine Corps. With that, they enlisted, and Lavaia's mother cried. "Old Italian women," he sighed. "She told my sisters there would be no pasta sauce made in the house until their brother came home."

Months after the Armistice was signed, Sergeant Lavaia said bluntly, "There was sniping going on. Don't let them tell you there wasn't. It wasn't over, really over." Even in the bitter cold, he made it a habit to keep the hood of his parka down, "so I could hear." The enemy, he explained, "wore these rubber-soled shoes, we called them Eedeewa Shoes, that didn't make any noise in the snow."

Sent directly to the Anti-Tank Company, Fifth Regiment, when he arrived, he remembered, "It was just getting dark when I got there. First thing, I got guard duty. I'd never walked my post in the middle of the night. Oh, my God, I thought I was going to die."

Two days later, in daylight, Lavaia had a much better introduction to Korea when he met up with Reckless. Still not known outside of the Marine Sector, she continued to startle, then charm the new guys in camp. "She was our friend," he said, remembering her knack for taking the guys' minds off the awfulness of where they were.

Patrolling for line crossers, whether enemy spies or displaced civilians, looking for snipers, going on forced marches, staying in shape with calisthenics, and cleaning weapons, "We followed routines. You didn't sit down, they wouldn't let you," Lavaia explained. Reckless continued, too, going on patrols and marches, same as the others. "We treated her like one of the Marines," he said.

A year after her extraordinary feats during the Battle for Outpost Vegas, Reckless was making the news again, written about in the March 31, 1954 edition of *The First Word*, the newsletter of the First Marine Division that came out every Friday. Instead of stories of her combat duty, they were humorous write-ups that, to some extent, may have reflected a relaxing attitude among the troops, even as they kept a watchful eye. Reckless, it turned out, made a poor food choice in trying to bite into a .30-caliber ammo clip, and the resulting loose teeth had to be treated with a saline rinse several times a day. The lighthearted article went on to list the many non-nutritional items she had eaten, as well as the many food indulgences fed to her by enlisted men and officers, alike.

A week later, *The First Word* reported that Reckless was missing. Unlike the unnerving episode when she disappeared soon after arriving on base, this time the scare was brief. The guys were just beginning to get worried when a ransom note appeared, obviously delayed long enough for the proper effect. The Anti-Tankers were in stand-by reserve about three miles north of the Imjin River, and a couple of miles down the road from another Fifth Regiment company, the 4.2 Mortars. Naturally, it made for conflicting stories: the Four Deuces, as the mortar company was called, claimed that Reckless had wandered into their camp. Not so, said her buddies, she was stolen. She, apparently, did not care much.

"They hijacked her," said Lavaia, scoffing at the fuss. "We knew right away they took her. They wanted money for a relief fund, so we kicked in and got her back." Treated like royalty during her "captivity," it was reported that Reckless' first meal was a platter of hotcakes. But when her hosts found out how much more she would happily eat, they pressed their demands. The Four Deuces wanted $400.00—and the sooner, the better or a feed bill might get attached, some must have thought. The outfit had its eye on divisional honors for the most money contributed to the Marine Memorial Fund drive for the benefit of the Iwo Jima memorial. Assuming the subterfuge worked, when the Anti-Tankers and their Recoilless Rifle Platoon paid up to get their horse returned, it would put the Four Deuces in the lead. Reckless' buddies had already contributed to the fund, but with payday coming up in a couple of days, they put together the ransom and home she came. Meanwhile, well aware that only the best would do for their kidnapped celebrity as they waited for their money, her hosts fed Reckless as much as she wanted—with no more disparaging remarks made about her appetite.

By the following Saturday, April 10, 1954, the hijinks involving the Four Deuces had given way to serious business in the Anti-Tank Company. Corporal Reckless was to be promoted to sergeant. A low platform was built, the company area cleaned up, the Marine Corps and national colors obtained from Headquarters Company, and in the warming April weather, unquestionably, Reckless was given a bath. On hand for the formal ceremony were Colonel Elby Martin, commander of the Fifth Regiment, and General Randolph McCall Pate, commander of the First Marine Division.

The company fell in, and General Pate trooped the line, after which Reckless, looking smart in her scarlet and gold blanket, and accompanied by a fellow Marine on either side, walked forward to the platform. Master Sergeant John Strange, the company's senior non-commissioned officer, read the following citation, fed through a megaphone for all to hear:

"For meritorious achievement in connection with operations against the enemy while serving with a Marine infantry in Korea from October 26, 1952 to July 27, 1953, Corporal Reckless performed the duties of ammunition carrier in a superb manner. Reckless' attention and devotion to duty makes her well qualified for promotion to the rank of sergeant. Her absolute dependability while on missions under fire contributed materially to the success of many battles."

After Sergeant Strange finished, General Pate pinned the chevrons on the blanket of his favorite warhorse. Also on her blanket were the two Purple Hearts for wounds sustained during the Battle for Outpost Vegas and, in addition, a Good Conduct Medal, the Presidential Unit Citation with Star, the National Defense Service Medal, the Korean Service Medal, the United Nations Service Medal, and the Republic of Korea Presidential Unit Citation, all of which the members of the platoon wore. On the left shoulder of her blanket was the French fourragere, worn by every member of the Fifth Regiment. The battle decoration is displayed in recognition of the regiment's heroic deeds of valor in World War I, as authorized by the French Ministry of War.

After the ceremony, Pate hosted a party for the Anti-Tank Company. Reckless' exploits were well known to the general, and he was an unabashed fan of hers, for what he called her esprit de corps. Pate left Korea the following month to become Assistant Commandant of the Marine Corps. By the time he and Reckless met again, he was the Corps' Commandant.

——— 5 ———

Surrounded by her buddies after the ceremony, Sergeant Reckless basked in their praise and broad smiles. She had made history, by virtue of what she had accomplished in battle, and the Fifth Regiment was proud to honor her achievements with the promotion to sergeant. Her Marines liked to say that she was the only horse who came out of the Korean War with fame and a name. Certainly, it was war and the needs of a regiment that set the stage for what Reckless did. Yet, it was her almost uncanny independence in the way she functioned in battle, in sync with her buddies, that distinguishes her from other warhorses known to history. Whether she was unique, we can never be sure. But among warhorses whose stories have been written, she was one of a kind.

The many others whose names are remembered, were all ridden in battle. Brave, physically strong, able to endure hardship, they were the favorites of military leaders in wars past. The partnerships were long lasting—cemented by that unique combination of personalities—and they were often lauded in written word and paintings, poetry, and song.

Starting in antiquity, perhaps the greatest horse was the massive Bucephalus, who captivated a 13-year-old Alexander the Great, in 344 B.C., after his father, King Philip II of Macedonia, refused to buy the unruly beast. Sensing that the horse was unnerved by his own shadow, Alexander turned him into the sun and spoke soothingly to him, eventually taming him and bringing him to hand. When he finally could ride Bucephalus, Philip was so impressed with his son's accomplishment that he told him to look beyond their homeland to a kingdom worthy of his greatness. The mighty charger served Alexander through many conflicts until, in 326 B.C., at 30 years old he succumbed to battle wounds.

The Chinese warlord Lü Bu rode Red Hare in battles toward the end of the Eastern Han Dynasty, an era that stretched from A.D. 25 to A.D. 220, and extended its influence south to Korea and Viet Nam. Based on mentions of him in historical texts, Red Hare was a very imposing horse described as well suited to long gallops and powerful leaps. He was an inspiring subject for fiction and painting, and is immortalized by the line, "Among men, Lü Bu; among horses, Red Hare," from the warlord's biography,

In 11th century Spain, the nobleman Rodrigo Diaz de Vivar, immortalized as El Cid, took as his trusted mount the Andalusian stallion, Babieca, through 30 years of military campaigns mostly in the service of the Spanish kings. Legends abound, from contrasting stories of Babieca's breeding to the pair's final ride, the dead El Cid strapped upright on his warhorse, riding into battle to the terror of the Spaniard's enemies. Many statues pay tribute to rider and horse, including one outside the cathedral where they are buried, in Burgos, Spain.

In Latin America, General Simon Bolivar's favorite horse was the gift of a peasant woman who, so the story goes, dreamt that some day she would give a famous general a horse she had raised. Palomo, named by Bolivar because its gray color reminded him of a cock pigeon, was the general's mount through the battle that liberated present-day Colombia from Spanish rule, in 1819. As testament to Palomo's favor with Bolivar, it is his shoes that are in a museum display with the general's effects.

George Washington, a superb horseman, had other mounts at his disposal but chose to ride the 16-hand charger, Nelson, most often during the American Revolution. A mature horse of about 15 years when he was given to the general by a friend, he proved to be the steadiest of Washington's horses in battle. He was the general's mount when the British army, under Lord Cornwallis, surrendered to Washington at Yorktown, Virginia, in 1781. Post war, Nelson enjoyed many years as a riding horse and then in complete retirement at Mount Vernon before his death in 1790.

Marengo, a small, gray Arabian imported from Egypt, was the Emperor Napoleon Bonaparte's enduring mount. Steady, courageous, and reliable, the horse was wounded eight times, yet served his master through many battles, including Napoleon's last, the Battle of Waterloo, in 1815. Through that same siege, the ultimately victorious Duke of Wellington commanded troops from astride another famous warhorse, his prized Copenhagen. The Thoroughbred-Arabian mix had enjoyed a respectable racing career before becoming the Duke's favorite mount. In 1846, the Duke and his horse were immortalized as the largest equestrian statue of its time in Great Britain.

As wars produce personalities, the American Civil War was no exception, generating its share of both men and the horses who gained fame with their masters. The Confederate commander, Robert E. Lee, looked upon the iron gray Traveller (spelled as the English do) as his favorite warhorse. He was said to have great stamina and, for the most part, was unflappable, save an incident during the Second Battle of Bull Run, in 1862, when he was spooked by advancing Union troops, and injured General Lee, who was standing beside him. Traveller was the general's mount when he surrendered at Appomattox Court House in Virginia, on April 9, 1865. He remained with Lee until the general's death, in 1870, after which the horse lived one year longer. Also riding for the Confederacy in the Civil War was Little Sorrel, the preferred mount of General Thomas "Stonewall" Jackson. A Morgan of average size at about 15 hands, the horse was a tireless campaigner, often carrying the general as many as 40 miles in a day. He was fearless, steady, and a comfortable ride for a horseman of modest ability, and he was with Jackson until the latter's death, due to complications from injuries sustained as the result of a volley fired by his own men during the Battle of Chancellorsville, in 1863.

Lieutenant General Ulysses S. Grant accepted General Lee's surrender at Appomattox on his large and powerful Thoroughbred, Cincinnati. A fine horseman who owned many horses during his life, Grant favored Cincinnati throughout the Civil War. He let almost no one ride the horse except a boyhood friend who had saved Grant's life, and Abraham Lincoln, who spent the last month of the war with Grant, and rode Cincinnati every day. In virtually all depictions of Grant on horseback, it is Cincinnati he is riding.

Then there was Comanche, a part Mustang, part Morgan horse who earned his name for his bravery in 1868, when the U.S. Army was fighting the Comanche Indians in Kansas. Even after a hindquarter was pierced with an arrow, he allowed his owner, Captain Myles Keogh, to stay mounted and continue to fight. Comanche's toughness never faltered, through several injuries and, finally, the disastrous Battle of Little Bighorn, in 1876. Surviving the battle in which all members of the U.S. Army Seventh Cavalry perished, he was found severely wounded two days later. Nursed back to health, he lived out his life in retirement, first at Fort Meade, South Dakota and later, Fort Riley, Kansas, where he was made the Second Commanding Officer of the Seventh Cavalry, a post he held until he died at about age 29, in 1891. The old warrior, it turned out, had a liking in common with Reckless. Whenever the opportunity presented itself, Comanche, too, indulged a fondness for beer.

And in World War I, the last war to function with horsepower, Warrior gained renown as the steadfast mount of Lieutenant Colonel Jack Seely through all the major battles of the Western Front. In 1918, Warrior and Seely, then commander of the Canadian Cavalry Brigade, stood in northern France before 1,000 mounted horses whose victorious charge stemmed the German Spring Offensive. Through a war that saw the demise of some eight million horses and mules, Warrior cheated death several times and earned the descriptive, "The horse the Germans couldn't kill." It was the headline for his obituary in London's *Evening Standard* when Warrior died on his native Isle of Wight in 1941, at age 33.

As great warhorses are remembered so, indeed, is what Reckless did for the Marines, her extraordinary bravery and the lives she saved during the Korean War. For that, she takes her place in a small and elite group. Yet, in conversations, what was always treasured were the warmhearted, often comic stories about the togetherness between Reckless and her buddies. "She was our friend," Mike Lavaia would say, time and again. His fondest memory of her happened one very hot day, the last summer the Fifth Regiment was in Korea.

The Marines were at mess, eating at the long tables. The tent flaps were rolled up all the way around. Reckless sauntered over and stuck her head under the tent roll, edging her head between two of the guys, who were hunched over their plates, chowing down.

"Yep, she stuck her head in there like she owned the place," recalled Lavaia. "She knew where to come to eat." Someone said, "Reckless is here." No one even looked up, they just slid a plate of food down to her. Maybe someone added, "Here you go," but that would have been it. She just started eating, alongside her buddies.

Chapter Seven

CALIFORNIA HERE SHE COMES

————— 1 —————

UAscom City, the enormous depot that had been processing incoming troops since the early stages of the war, had reversed its engines. From the start of the buildup, almost a million men had moved through the compound, arriving on ships three thousand or more at a time. But by the fall of 1954, the far bigger job was sending them home. Trucked from their units to the railroad head at Munsan-ni, then riding the old, slow train between there and the depot, troops were packed up and outward bound.

Someone remembered being roused by Debbie Reynolds singing, "Good Morning," from the movie, *Singing in the Rain*, with Gene Kelly. For the guys who were heading home, it had a ring of truth: they had survived Korea; it was a good morning. Most of them spent three days at the depot, working their way through the exiting process, and enjoying the amenities of clean tents, hot meals and showers, movies, a PX shop, and a service club. They also put up with treatment for lice and worms, at the military's insistence that such vermin were best left in Korea, and not transported elsewhere. However, in short order they were all on buses headed for Inchon harbor and to many of the same ships that had brought them over. With bittersweet good-byes, and promises to stay in touch, they were on their way home.

Reckless was still awaiting her rotation orders—and no one was sure what would happen to her. Lieutenant Pedersen and Sergeant Latham had both agreed that every effort should be made to get her to the states, but nothing definite had been worked out. The guys had wanted to buy Reckless from Pedersen before he left Korea, but he felt his money had been well spent and he didn't want to be repaid. Nevertheless, for all intents and purposes, with Pedersen gone she belonged to the men of the Fifth Regiment's Recoilless Rifle Platoon. And there was no way in hell those guys were going to leave her behind.

Just how they were going to get her to the U.S. was another matter. She was not, as they termed it, military issue—and that was the sticking point. Correspondence with Marine Corps headquarters in Washington, D.C. attempting to find a way to get her to the states, ultimately proved fruitless. The military's hands were tied. Reckless had been purchased with private funds, and while she was attached to the Marine Corps, she was not owned by the Corps, and the concern was that the use of government funds to transport her could be seen as engaging in a commercial venture.

What would happen to her? Many of the guys headed home not knowing. Paul Hammersley, among them, hated to think of the outcome if she was left behind. Her future in a starving country, struggling to get back on its feet, was not bright. Of his leave taking, he said, "It's a happy day, but it's also a sad day, because some of these friends you'll never see again." The trucks came into the compound, and everyone who was going was packed and ready. Reckless was not around, and Hammersley did not go looking for her. "I guess I didn't want to see her. You know, sometimes it's hard to say good-bye."

It took time and some maneuvering, but eventually a solution took shape. Lieutenant Colonel Andrew Geer, a former commander of the Second Battalion, Fifth Regiment, the unit for which Reckless had spent nights hauling mortar rounds during the Battle for Vegas, headed home in December 1953. A screenwriter and author, he quickly wrote an article about Reckless for the *Saturday Evening Post* that ran the following April, sparking readers' interest, including that of Stan Coppel, executive vice president of the States Steamship Line.

In August 1954, States acquired the Pacific Transport Line, with its lucrative route of East Asian ports of call. Pacific had considerable experience transporting animals and, in fact, just the year before, the SS Washington, one of the States Steamship vessels, had carried a baby elephant named Rosy from Thailand to Portland, Oregon, to fill a void at the Portland Zoo. It had never had an elephant, and a gift from two local residents living in Thailand would change that. A publicity campaign raised $5,000.00 for Rosy's transportation, but J.R. Dant, the head of States, told the zoo to use the money for her quarters instead, and gave her free passage. Now, a year later, Dant backed Coppel's suggestion to bring Reckless from Yokohama, Japan to San Francisco, California, on the SS Pacific Transport. Since States' ships had served the military during the Korean War, it was certainly a nice touch at war's end for one of its ships to step up and give free passage to a war hero.

That left one more wrinkle to be ironed out: how to get Reckless from Korea to Yokohama. However, the debate about whether or not she was going was over. It was now just a matter of working out the logistics. Her ship passage was set; she was going to the states. A letter from Major General Robert E. Hogaboom, commander of the First Marine Division, to the First Marine Aircraft Wing, inquired about the possibility of flying Reckless to Yokohama. The reply indicated the Marines would consider it a challenge to airlift the first livestock in the R4Q Flying Boxcar, henceforth called Operation Horse Shift. There appeared to be no further paper trail. On the designated day, Reckless was trucked to Kimpo Airfield, where she flew out on the first leg of her journey to California.

Her last morning in camp, like clockwork, Reckless waited for Sergeant John Meyers to get her pancakes. It had been a daily ritual for the last year, ever since Meyers, among the last wave of Marines coming into Korea, arrived in November 1953. A Philadelphia native, he was influenced by his older brother, who had been on Iwo Jima, and joined the Marines right out of high school. He had heard that the Fifth Regiment had a horse before he arrived at Camp Casey, but did not think anymore about it until Reckless introduced herself.

A recoilless rifleman on patrols, Meyers pulled mess duty in reserve. The mess hall was one of Reckless' favorite haunts, and when she spied the new guy, she went up and gave him a nudge. "I didn't know what to think," he chuckled, but it got her a stack of pancakes rustled up by Manny, the cook. "He was this big guy from Brooklyn," Meyers recalled. "He could cook good pancakes and, boy, did Reckless like them. She had some appetite."

She could also be cunning in how she positioned herself for best results. Meyers had been schooled in the fine art of table setting by his older sisters, which got him the added job of setting tables in the upstairs officers' mess. His morning route took him out the back of the mess hall to a flight of stairs—at the foot of which Reckless waited every morning. When Meyers went on patrol with the Recoilless Rifle Platoon, if she was not going with them, she would accept pancakes from a designated stand-in. Perhaps if Meyers had thought to remind someone on his day off, it would have been okay. But a slip-up did not go unnoticed. Reckless found his tent and the sleeping Meyers. Using her well-honed tactic, she bit his arm to wake him, then looked down at the bleary-eyed Marine as if to say, "Where are my pancakes?"

Meyers never saw Reckless after she left Korea. But like the rest of the Marines who were still there, the ones who liked to say, "We turned the lights out," he knew she had made it to California. He remembered her as his buddy, and always said she left a lasting impression on him. "Sometimes, you'd swear she knew what you were thinking. You know, she'd get this funny look on her face, almost like she was reading your mind."

2

Football season was underway among the services in Korea, and on October 17, 1954, the game between the First Marine Division and the Seventh Army Division had an unusual halftime show: the rotation ceremony for Sergeant Reckless. Backed by the formality of the regimental colors, and the panache of a drum and bugle corps, division commander General Hogaboom read a tribute extolling Reckless' bravery and dedication to the Marine Corps. The honoree, dressed in her scarlet blanket, stood quietly beside her new handler, Private First Class William Moore. Her ears flipping back and forth said clearly that she was absorbing all that was going on. A few days later, loaded in the same type of utility trailer hitched behind a jeep, that had taken her many places in the Western Sector, she headed for Kimpo Airfield, about 35 miles west of Seoul. Moore would accompany Reckless to California, his ship passage paid for by the Marines.

Waiting for her at the airfield was an R4Q Flying Boxcar, a large, boxy aircraft with high-set wings that could take on dozens of paratroopers or an assortment of jeeps and other large cargo with ease. If flying a horse was a new experience for the First Marine Aircraft Wing, the how-to information was available. Horsemen had been flying racehorses between tracks of appreciable distance for the better part of a decade, and with experience it was becoming more routine.

Cargo, which rather unceremoniously Reckless was considered, loaded through the rear of the fuselage, up a ramp that cantilevered down from the plane's floor. Once inside, she would have walked into a safety pen, essentially a topless wooden crate, comfortable enough for her to stand in but not move about. Kimpo to Yokohama, Japan, was a short flight, about two hours, and she likely would have made it without food or water. Indeed, as calm and steady as she usually was, if someone had found her dozing, it would not have been a surprise.

The SS Pacific Transport arrived in Yokohama on October 25, 1954, its hold already full of fish, mostly large albacore tuna picked up at several ports along its route. It was a Type C-3 freighter, the largest of the freighter classes commissioned during World War II, and one of the last built, in 1945. Before leaving California waters, it had gone to Los Angeles and back up to Stockton, then headed westward on September 8, to stops at Honolulu, Hawaii, three ports in Japan, two in the Philippines, and Hong Kong. Then, turning homeward, it made four more stops in Japan, the last being the Port of Yokohama where the crew picked up Reckless.

It was a 24-hour stopover, and in that short time, Marines came on board to build Reckless' stall, and load on straw bedding, food, and a salt lick. Her quarters amounted to a small cabin with the top half of the front side left open, and a sloping roof pitched to the back. It was set behind the wheelhouse on the starboard side of the deck, a position that gave its occupant the best protection from the elements and plenty of fresh air. The return trip was to take ten days, though the projected arrival in San Francisco was understood to be approximate. Given the number of stops and potential for delay, the reality was that freighters arrived when they made port. And in this case, they still had to make another stop in northern Japan, to take on more fish at the port of Otaru.

Reckless came aboard on October 26, hoisted from the pier to the ship's port deck in a safety crate similar to the one she traveled in during her flight from South Korea. She settled into shipboard life easily, in extremely capable hands. The Pacific Transport Line had brought an assortment of new animals for the Tokyo Zoo after World War II and, more recently, sheep and cattle to replenish the herds in South Korea. James Burneson, the refrigeration maintenance man on the ship—"reefers," they were called—had seen firsthand what poor travelers some animals could be, and was impressed with Reckless from the start. Indeed, the Able Bodied Seaman who was assigned to her care, and who was a rancher when he was not at sea, thought she was the easiest horse he had ever worked with.

Burneson first went to sea in 1944, signing on for his initial voyage not long after he was sent home to St. Louis, Missouri, his hopes for being a Marine ended when it was found that he turned 16 in boot camp. Drafted into the Army during the early part of the Korean War, he spent his time as a radio operator on loan to other services, including several months with the Marines' First Amphibious Tractor Battalion. Resuming his seagoing career in 1952, Burneson also continued his practice of keeping a detailed diary of every voyage he made, recollections that illuminated Reckless' time at sea.

Leaving Otaru, Japan before the end of October, the SS Pacific Transport set course for San Francisco via the Northern Circle route, crossing the International Dateline on November 4. Reckless continued to be the perfect passenger—friendly, calm, seemingly unfazed by the working ship's environment. Almost apologetically, Burneson noted that she was simply nothing special on a ship that had already carried such a varied assortment of four-legged passengers.

Nevertheless, Reckless wore the mantle of the Marine Fifth Regiment, and while her presence had the blessing of the ship's captain, Kenneth Shannon, the weight of who she was also rested on his shoulders. A Navy veteran and highly respected ship's master who had captained the Pacific

Transport for a number of years, Shannon ran a tight ship, and the crews that sailed with him were expected to tow the line. Posting a sign on her stall requesting that she not be bothered was in keeping with the captain's style and his concern for Reckless' well being. Fortunately for the VIP horse, no one took the notice too literally and she, in turn, was happy with a hello from anyone who passed by. Whether or not she ever met the captain's cocker spaniels, of which there were always several on board, was never reported.

Horsemen would have described Reckless as an easy shipper, her only apparent vice being her mischievous gobbling of any pack of cigarettes she could get at. Everyone, Burneson included, soon learned to keep their smokes pocketed and not set them down untended on the sill of her stall. "She had a sense of humor," he chuckled, "and she loved attention, just loved it. She thought people were her friends, and were there to take care of her."

Other than disappearing cigarettes, Burneson's log indicated that the trip was uneventful, with calm seas throughout, refuting an earlier, invented story about the ship hitting a typhoon. Archaic weather charts also indicated that no foul weather interfered with the Pacific Transport's crossing. A day out from port, the uneventful part changed, however, when Reckless chewed up her scarlet and gold blanket. Living in an on-deck stall, she had been kept warm throughout the trip with a more durable, everyday blanket, but the plan was that she would disembark wearing her scarlet and gold one. Burneson recalled someone trying it on her, then theorized that it was left within her reach once the other blanket had been put back on. It was as good as gone.

No one saw her shredding it, of course, but Burneson happened by when Moore was heading off with what was left of the blanket. "We're going to have a helluva time with this damn thing," he remembered Moore saying, though without the least reproach toward Reckless. To himself, Burneson always savored the episode. "It caused problems," he admitted, "but it was so comic. Among the Marines are mavericks, and I think she fitted in very well." It fell to Captain Shannon to make the unpleasant call to the Marines, that with little time remaining, they would need to find Reckless a new blanket, and it would need all new decorations.

3

As Reckless headed to California, her imminent arrival was being chronicled. Bob Considine, International News Service columnist and radio talk show host, kept up a commentary about her on his daily radio show, and on November 5, 1954 filed a story that was picked up by *Stars and Stripes* in the Far East and Europe. Herb Caen wrote about her with the cutline, *Celebrity Note*, in his daily column of local goings-on and gossip, "Baghdad By The Bay," in the *San Francisco Examiner*. California Governor Goodwin J. Knight issued a proclamation applauding her courage and welcoming her to the state. And Ed Sullivan, equally taken with Reckless' story, devoted his "Little Old New York" column to her in New York's *Sunday News* for November 7. With Pacific Transport adhering to the give-or-take-a-few-days schedule of freighters, her arrival date was still unsure. As the stated date of November 5 passed, so did Ed Sullivan's apparent hope to have a crew film her arrival, then fly the footage to New York for airing on his Sunday night variety show. He also tendered the offer to fly her east to appear live on his show but that, too, did not pan out. It was certainly an entertainment loss, as Reckless would have been a natural for the show, with Sullivan's unabashed love of real life heroes. And by the end of 1954, Sullivan's hugely popular CBS show was pulling upwards of ten million viewers every week.

On the coast, Lieutenant Pedersen headed from Camp Pendleton to San Francisco, this time with a conventional horse trailer in tow, a loan from the base stables. His wife, Katherine, remembered her husband's surprise at receiving orders to meet a ship that was bringing Reckless to the U.S. After Korea, he never expected to see her again. Other buddies from the war years also headed to the city, including one of her former handlers, Monroe Coleman, who drove from his home in Utah.

Alerted to the news that Reckless' Korean silk blanket was beyond redemption, Pedersen arrived to find a replacement. One of the bay area's better-known saddleries, Olsen Nolte, stepped up to the plate, donating a lighter covering, more appropriate to California weather. The shop even managed to have the lettering, "Sgt. Reckless" and under that, "1st Mar. Div." sewn on the sides in rapid time, but adding her sergeant's stripes, her Purple Hearts and other war decorations would have to wait.

It was late afternoon on November 9, 1954, when the SS Pacific Transport sailed under the Golden Gate Bridge, steered by a harbor pilot to its berth at pier 7 along The Embarcadero. The bridge's roadway lights were on, and the massive orange structure would have caused a momentary darkness as its shadow moved across the deck. But Reckless would have understood nothing of the iconic symbol and what it meant to the countless servicemen who sailed under it, going to war and then returning, first in World War II and then the Korean War. Had she known, she might have felt the same as Jack Nelmark, whose mortar crew she supplied the nights they battled for Outpost Vegas.

"Over the years, whenever I've seen that bridge, I think, man, you were lucky to get out of that," he said. Coming into San Francisco around midnight, he remembered there weren't any troops below deck. "We were all up on deck, cheering. And all those people on the pier cheering, too. Boy, oh, boy, that was really something." He wished he had told his wife to come to San Francisco. Instead, they met in Chicago, then went home to Wisconsin where Nelmark picked up where he left off, resuming his job with the Wausau Paper Company.

The drizzle had stopped by the time they docked at 5:15 p.m. Too late for the crew to sign off in front of the shipping commissioner, as the latter was gone for the day at 5:00 p.m., it meant all stayed on board another night. An inspector from the Department of Agriculture came on the ship to draw blood samples from Reckless for two mandatory tests, both for contagious equine diseases: glanders, a disease of the respiratory track, lungs, and skin; and dourine, a venereal disease. Had the tests come back positive, Reckless would have been sent right back to South Korea. The negative results, when they came from the laboratory, prompted wisecracks about a diet laced with cigarettes, John Wayne cookies, and beer helping to keep her healthy. Meanwhile, in the morning restrictions were lifted and she was given temporary clearance to leave the ship.

Whether it was pure luck, or the captain's careful maneuvering, November 10, the day Reckless actually stepped onto U.S. soil was the official birthday of the Marine Corps. The weather in San Francisco was fair and a little warmer than usual for that time of year.

Reckless had early visitors—Pedersen and Coleman, to get her ready to depart—and a surprised Maureen Shannon, the captain's daughter, who was always one of the first on board when her father's ship came in. She still remembers her delight in meeting Reckless, though laughingly admits that to a nine-year-old, Reckless did not seem small at all.

There was no sheet, the light covering for Reckless to wear, as yet. Delayed no doubt for the lettering to be affixed, it meant all available hands likely pitched in to brush, comb, spot-shampoo, and generally spruce up the famous warhorse for her press debut. And indeed, they were waiting— a pier full of reporters and photographers from the wire services and local media including, as testament to how the story had grown, the

San Francisco Examiner and the *San Francisco Chronicle.*

Much as she had begun her trip from Yokohama, Reckless soared through the air in a safety crate. This time, swung wide from a boom on the ship's deck, and lowered by cables and the steadying hands of longshoremen, her crate settled on the pier below. Pedersen took the brief flight with her, and once the front panel of the topless box had been opened, the two Marines walked out together.

Flash bulbs popped, reporters shouted questions, and Reckless stood happily soaking up the attention as her fellow Marines answered for her. Besides Pedersen and Coleman, Sergeant Elmer Lively had driven from Camp Pendleton; and Andrew Geer, in the midst of writing a book about Reckless, was on home turf. Joe Latham, stationed at Camp Lejeune in South Carolina, had tried his best, but couldn't make the trip.

San Franciscans did not read the story until the following morning, when the two daily newspapers gave the unusual arrival major coverage. "Sgt. Reckless, Famed Korean Filly, Arrives," said the *Chronicle*, relating her exploits in two columns plus a picture of Coleman feeding her a carrot. Said the *Examiner* headline over an equally long story, "Marine Sgt. Reckless Lands Here—On All 4 [sic]." Both covered her war record, plus her busy and unusual day on the town.

4

After her morning meet-and-greet with the press, Reckless and her entourage headed for the Marines' Memorial Club, only a short ride from the pier. Even in weekday traffic, the jeep with horse trailer behind made its way easily to the Beaux Arts-style building at the corner of Sutter and Mason Streets. The private hotel and social club housed there counts as its members U.S. Marines and other veterans of the U.S. armed forces. It was conceived as a "living memorial" to Marine casualties of the World War II/War in the

Pacific, and was opened on the Marine Corps birthday in 1946.

Eight years later, it would welcome a most unexpected guest who would, without even trying, command center stage three times in the one day. That afternoon, Reckless and her party held another press event, this one on the stage of the club's theater, a well-known venue that dates to the original 1926 building. Her new sheet had been delivered before they left the pier, and she was wearing it as she stood on stage. Questions, answers, and more photographs filled the allotted time, including some shots of Reckless enjoying a liquid refreshment. As the story goes, one of the Marines was quick to realize that Coca-Cola, with its amber color, could be misconstrued as something less wholesome, so milk was substituted as her beverage of choice.

The main event that night celebrated the 179th birthday of the Marine Corps, established on November 10, 1775, when the Second Continental Congress, in Philadelphia, Pennsylvania, decreed that the American colonies would have such an armed force. Though November 10 did not become the official birthday until 1921, thereafter it was made a holiday, celebrated every year by Marines the world over with a traditional ball and cake cutting. Even when conditions prevent a full-scale celebration the day is always honored, as did Lieutenant Colonel Lewis B. "Chesty" Puller in Korea. On November 10, 1950, during a brief lull in the Chosin Campaign, he sliced a cake, delighting his men, so one story went, by using a captured North Korean saber.

In San Francisco, four years later, the event had all the trimmings of the prescribed celebration—music, fine food, dancing, and one thing more: Reckless as the guest of honor. She arrived in the banquet hall in time for dessert, and readily accepted the first piece of cake from Katherine Pedersen. As Blaine Myers quipped some years later, remembering her success in grabbing his cupcakes in Korea, "I would have liked to see them keep the cake from her." As everyone applauded and savored the moment,

Reckless gracefully turned and began munching the flowers on the dais—that, too, delighting the 400 assembled guests.

Later that evening, she repeated her letter-perfect performance, riding the elevator to the 10th floor Crystal Ballroom for the traditional cake-cutting ceremony. At 10:00 p.m., a huge cake glowing with 179 lighted candles was wheeled into the room. Again, Katherine Pedersen did the honors, this time offering Reckless the first piece of cake as the most honored Marine present. Tradition also says that the first piece goes to the youngest Marine present and, at age five, she was that. The Lieutenant had sent home a number of photos of Reckless, though in real life she turned out to be smaller than Mrs. Pedersen thought she would be. "But she was just as beautiful," she said.

As the star of the evening, even if an equine version, Reckless comported herself with the utmost finesse through both appearances, a marvel to many in attendance. It was as if being the guest of honor was a perfectly reasonable thing for a horse to do. But it had been a very long day, filled with all sorts of newness, and she needed to rest. Pedersen vanned her back to the docks, where a stall had been reserved. Presumably, a holding stall for incoming horses, for one very tired Reckless, it would do fine.

After posing for countless photos, standing alertly while she was talked about, and in all other ways holding it together for a day of pomp and ceremony, Reckless woke up on Wednesday morning needing to blow off a little steam. Lieutenant Pedersen, wise horseman, was thinking the same thing. Finding out that the Cow Palace would be a hospitable venue, the pair headed out to the big indoor arena that straddles the border between San Francisco and Daly City. It had its own military history, as a staging area for troops heading for the Pacific Theater during World War II, and Reckless galloping around for a little while brought a bit of reminiscence to the interlude.

It also refreshed her for one more noteworthy appearance. In the afternoon, Reckless was a guest at the resolutely all-male membership Bohemian Club, and as Katherine Pedersen noted, "the only four-legged lady to ever be served a drink there." Nothing, really, is known about the visit, but a photograph showed Elmer Lively and Pedersen ushering Reckless through a door into the carpeted interior. The private club on Taylor Street had been a haven for journalists, artists, and musicians for years after its founding in 1872, but over time came to include members from many more professions. While they could not have offered a female membership, Reckless' visit certainly supported their inclusive attitude.

Fresh from a second night stabled at the pier, Reckless was loaded into the horse van and she and Lieutenant Pedersen, and likely Sergeant Lively, headed to Camp Pendleton, nearly 500 miles south. It was a much longer ride than anything Reckless had experienced, and Pedersen stopped frequently to give her water and light snacks. Ahead was one more formal occasion, the last for a while, they could have assured her.

Reckless delighted her host, Major General John T. Selden describing her beauty and good manners to be just as he was told to expect. The commanding general of Camp Pendleton was on hand at the front gate to meet the new arrival, and in a brief welcoming ceremony signed the guestbook for Reckless. Photographs recorded her watching intently as Selden's hand moved across the page, as if she understood exactly what was going on. It was the same look that had prompted her buddies to talk of her knowing, almost mind-reading reactions they remembered so well.

Mrs. Selden wanted to meet Reckless, too, and the party moved on to the general's hacienda, in the historic Camp Margarita section of Pendleton. More photographs, more neck rubs and strokes, more smiles—on a beautiful day in the upper 60s, so unlike November in Korea, Sergeant Reckless was enjoying her favorite spot, at center stage.

Within a little more than three weeks, this tough little pony had traveled from Korea to California, experiencing her first plane flight and first voyage, making appearances for two days in San Francisco that would have flattered any celebrity, and finally taking a seven-hour road trip south to her new home. The topography in Southern California would remind her of her homeland, as all but winter would, too; and the food would be the same as her buddies had been feeding her the last two years. Her new home would be a comfortable fit, as Reckless would find out.

And as she would have said, had she had the words, "You were lucky, gal, lucky to have made it."

Chapter Eight

ANOTHER NEW LIFE

———— 1 ————

U The Marines came home from the Korean War, many of them going right back to the jobs they had left when they enlisted in the Corps. Still others started new lives, Reckless among them. A whirlwind two days in San Francisco, a stop at Camp Pendleton to meet the base commander, and then she was on to Vista, a few miles beyond the camp's southern boundary, where she would be the guest of Lieutenant and Mrs. Pedersen for the next year. Again benefitting from friends in high places, her stay at the Pedersen's ranch, would replace several months in a U.S. Department of Agriculture quarantine facility in San Francisco.

Testing their warhorse for infectious diseases when she had first landed, especially for dourine with its implication that Reckless had been "misbehaving," was insulting enough to her Marines. Keeping Reckless in quarantine was more than they could put up with. Governor Goodwin Knight's office concurred, and after the Pedersens offered to keep her on their five-acre spread for the extended period, she was settled in without further ado.

With her own pasture, and access to a small barn when she wanted cover, and the company of other horses and 4H animals nearby, it was a perfect fit. The couple's young children, Eric, Jr. and Katy, delighted in taking care of her, and on weekends, there were always visitors to see the famous Reckless. "There was quite a lot of publicity about her," Mrs. Pedersen remembered. "It was an interesting year."

In August, Pedersen, by then promoted to captain, began the process of moving her to Camp Pendleton, and on November 22, 1955, the final bill of sale was signed between him and the First Marine Division Association. Correspondence with Marine Corps Headquarters in Washington, D.C. confirmed that Pedersen had always retained ownership of Reckless, despite stories that persisted about the platoon members in Korea buying her. Now, he accepted one dollar from the First Marine Division Association and, with that, Reckless had new owners and soon, a new place to live.

Had Reckless been pregnant at the time, according to the contract, Captain Pedersen would have owned the foal. But she was not, and no future progeny ever went to him. When the Pedersens brought Reckless to Camp Pendleton, after the sale was completed, it was their last involvement with her for many years. Meanwhile, the new owners drafted a set of guidelines strictly governing any public appearances Reckless might make. Such requests had to be in writing, generous donations were expected for the Association's Scholarship Fund, and all ventures were to reflect positively on the Marine Corps and the First Division. Initially, there was some interest in using Reckless in public events that could promote the Corps, and in her first year at Pendleton, the Johnson & Higgins insurance agency wrote a $5,000.00 livestock policy for her protection. There was even talk of her appearing at the International Livestock Exposition in San Francisco at the end of October 1955. However, that didn't materialize, nor did any schedule of outside events. For whatever reason, through the years her appearances remained associated with Pendleton and her

Marines, involving activities either on the base or, if beyond, with the Fifth Regiment. The decision certainly reflected the high regard they had for Reckless and, as such, the care with which the Marines wanted her handled.

Reckless' new owners planned for her to live at the base stables, and she may well have done so for the first few months she was at Camp Pendleton. But her regiment had other plans. Befitting their beloved Reckless, the Fifth Marines settled her in her own stable, in the Camp Margarita section of Pendleton, down the hill from Regimental Headquarters and not far from the base commander's hacienda. Several of the guys who knew her post war remember her there, pampered by her Marines, and kept entertained by countless visitors who wanted to see the famous horse.

The guys built the barn especially for Reckless, remembered Staff Sergeant Larry Ames, from Portland, Oregon, a 12-year veteran who came to Pendleton in 1957. "Luxurious" was how he described her digs. "She was treated with the utmost care and attention. I mean, there were Marines who took care of her." And with concern for her back, that had carried so much weight in Korea, by order of the base commander, Reckless was never again to have anything heavier than a blanket on her back. Or as Ames recalled it, "You could pet her, you could lead her, you could feed her, but that was it." The times when someone would get on her for a leisurely walk or a short trot were over.

No question, the guys at Pendleton loved Reckless just as much as the guys had in Korea. They were also very proud of the private quarters they had provided. But something must have seemed different—perhaps she missed the constant closeness of so many of her buddies, or the freedom she had to roam about the compound. Or perhaps she missed the tents that she could duck into, or the mess hall where she got chow along with the others. Even though she had guys cleaning her stall, and making sure she had fresh water and hay, and her meals on time; even though she had plenty of visitors bringing apples and carrots, and cars to watch going by on Basilone Road, she was alone. That had never happened before. Not in the pasture on Jeju Island in Korea, where she ran with her herd. Not at the Seoul racetrack turned into an airfield, where racetrackers and their ponies hung out around the periphery, waiting for a better tomorrow. And certainly it had not happened at the front in Korea, where she was always not just near her buddies, but one of them.

So Reckless fixed things. Every couple of weeks, she would let herself out of her enclosure and visit the general's hacienda. It was not visible from her stable, but if she followed the road, it brought her there. Once arrived, she visited the general's own horses—just a hello in passing, but enough for them to loudly acknowledge her presence—and then she dined on the flowers planted by the general's wife. The general was not amused.

It was not long before the telephone rang at headquarters. Sergeant Bill Bleeks, of Norwalk, Connecticut, laughed at the memory of one such episode, as the duty non-commissioned officer answered the phone. Identifying himself and the Fifth Marines, the unlucky officer stood ramrod straight, as everyone else in the office doubled up with laughter.

"Yes, sir. ... No, sir. ... Yes, sir. ... Yes, sir."

"I understand. I'll repeat what you said, sir."

"Yes, sir. We are to send somebody down and get

that f---ing horse off your lawn."

"Yes, sir. I understand, sir. Right away, sir."

From the other end, the decibel of the general's voice could have been heard quite clearly without the use of a telephone. The master sergeant dispatched someone to retrieve their wayward pony, fully aware that soon enough they would be doing it again. It is a virtual certainty that not one cross word was ever uttered to Reckless' face. It was too funny, and everyone knew it. And though he never admitted it, perhaps even the general did.

The target of Reckless' mischief-making sorties is a picturesque and historic treasure, not just of Camp Pendleton but also of Southern California. Listed on the National Register of Historic Places since 1970, the sprawling rancho is a 22-acre complex that includes the main house, designed in the hacienda-style around an inner courtyard, a chapel, bunkhouse, laundry building, and several outbuildings. Begun in 1841 and added to in stages until 1916, it was used as the official residence of Pendleton's base commander until 2007, when new living quarters were completed and the rancho became a multi-use center.

The Marine base is carved out of the southern portion of the immense Rancho Santa Margarita y Las Flores, and is the last large tract of open land in the area between San Diego and Orange counties. The 125,000-acre spread was purchased in 1942 for close to $4.25 million, or $34.00 an acre. Its history is replete with missionaries and gamblers, saloonkeepers and cattlemen, who began shaping the area 250 years ago with the establishment of the mission system to convert the Indians to Christianity. Out of the two largest missions, San Juan Capistrano in the north, and San Luis Rey in the south, Rancho Santa Margarita y Las Flores was created.

Enter the Pico brothers—Don Pio Pico, the last Mexican governor of California, and Andre Pico, a captain in the Mexican army—both of whom were favorites of the Mexican government, and were awarded a large parcel of the Rancho Santa Margarita y Las Flores after the missions were secularized, beginning in 1833. Gamblers always heavily in debt, the Picos eventually ceded the land to their brother-in-law, Don Juan Forster, in exchange for him assuming their debts. However, Forster himself was forced into debt when his successful cattle enterprise was undercut by the uncertainties in the livestock market, and the costs imposed by California's new fencing regulations. Though he had hoped to protect his fortune by subdividing his great land holdings, the move was never made, and after his death, Forster's heirs were forced to sell the entire tract.

The next owners, James Flood, a San Francisco saloon owner who had made his money from the discovery of silver ore in Nevada's Comstock Lode, and his friend, Richard O'Neill, a successful cattleman from northern California, bought the Rancho Santa Margarita y Las Flores for $450,000.00. Flood supplied most of the money, and O'Neill and, later, his son worked the ranch, which they developed into a successful cattle enterprise. For the next 60 years or so, the owners presided over some 225,000 acres that stretched from just north of Oceanside to El Toro, another 35 miles up the California coast. Better than half of the southern end of the tract, from Oceanside north to San Clemente, is what became Camp Pendleton. In October 1944, it was designated as a permanent installation and in 1946, it became the home of the First Marine Division.

––––– **2** –––––

As an active-duty Marine, Reckless was front and center whenever the Fifth Regiment called, and extended marches—40 miles, 100 miles, even 150 miles—were part of the drill. Just how much of the distance she covered on foot is unclear, though press clippings and photos, not to mention firsthand accounts attested to her presence. Some said she marched the whole way, at least on the shorter marches, while others believed that she was trailered to various points. However, the men all agree on one thing: when the regiment marched through a town along its route, or marched back into Camp Pendleton, Reckless was at the front of the column, right behind the regimental colors, leading her Marines.

Ames was with her on a march that took the men on a 100-mile round trip from Pendleton to San Diego and back. Through the countryside, Reckless rode in her trailer, he remembered. But on the outskirts of every town on their route, big or small, they would halt while she was unloaded and brought to the head of the line, to lead the guys down main street. "You can imagine, here we go through a town of, say, 20,000. People are out on the street, cheering and making lots of noise, and it didn't bother her a bit," Ames said. Nor was she in the least fazed when the regiment reached the Marine Corps Recruit Depot in San Diego and the men were all together, some 5,000 strong. Again at the front, she was where her Marines wanted her to be.

These marches were also remembered with some Marine-style humor, as when men, exhausted from several days on foot in the sweltering California heat, had to wait at Pendleton's gates for their warhorse to get in position. Memories of "waiting for the damn horse to lead us in," were common, but always coupled with the add-on that Reckless was theirs and they were proud of it. Bill Bleeks had his own version of the waiting-for-Reckless stories. It was when the Marines did what he believed was their longest hike, 150 miles to 29 Palms, California and back to Pendleton. "We did 30 miles a day for five days," he said. "When we got back, they had Reckless there, and she came in with us. It was quite a show." And wherever he was in the formation, one bone-tired Bleeks admitted to also thinking, "Where the hell is she? I'm going to ride her the rest of the way."

Reckless was always good copy, and the press office at Camp Pendleton kept churning out the news releases. She appeared at Armed Forces Day events, and the frequent weekend rodeos. And each year, she led the grand entry parade at the base's all-important June rodeo to benefit Navy Relief. Reckless soaked up the attention, and after fulfilling her official duties, she did the same with beers that were poured into an upturned helmet hung in an opportune place. When she wanted a refill, she stood by the empty helmet until someone obliged, which they usually did.

She was on hand for the serious events, of course—regimental inspections, change of command ceremonies, and retirements. "I thought of the times she would be out in front of the regiment," Ames said. "She would be standing there, the band would be playing The Marine Corps Hymn, and there would be dignitaries all around. She just stood there, very much a lady, and took it all in." She knew she was special, he agreed. "I have no doubt of it."

Amidst all of those paying attention to her, Reckless had one special friend, Master Sergeant Alford Lee McLaughlin, from Leeds, Alabama, one of 42 Marines who received the Congressional Medal of Honor for service during the Korean War. Lee, as he liked being called, was with Item Company, Third Battalion, Fifth Regiment, in Korea when, during the attack on Outpost Bruce (later Reno) in September 1952, he was responsible for killing 150 Communist Chinese and wounding an estimated 50 more, alternately firing two machine guns, his carbine, and hand grenades pulled from enemy dead.

At Camp Pendleton, in the later 1950s, fellow Marines remembered the special bond McLaughlin had with Reckless, a clear connection between two war heroes. He was devoted to her, and could usually be spotted around her stall—mucking it out, or giving her a rubdown. Some of the guys even thought he may have been billeted nearby. They recalled a private person who did not want any recognition, only to take care of Reckless, as his other duties allowed. They did pose for a newspaper photographer once, and when the picture ran, the caption noted, "They're the best of friends."

As she settled into a quieter, post-war life, the idea of Reckless having a family took hold and, in the spring of 1957, she produced her first offspring, a gray colt by a Thoroughbred sire. The birth, on Saturday evening, April 6, prompted the Fifth Regiment to hold a naming contest, which was won by Private First Class Robert E. Gibbs, who suggested the name Fearless. Two years later, on March 5, 1959, Reckless had another gray colt, this one sired by the Arabian stallion, Amyr Rasr. Again, there was a naming contest, though when none of the submissions measured up to the expectations of the Fifth Regiment's commander, he made his own choice and named the colt Dauntless.

Five years later, in 1964, Reckless had a third son, Chesty, seal brown in color and from the same Thoroughbred that sired Fearless. He was named after General Lewis B. "Chesty" Puller. The general never met Reckless in Korea, having left the war zone well before she showed up, nor is it known if he ever met his namesake. After Chesty, there was one more offspring, in 1965, this time a filly, sired by a registered Quarter Horse. Sadly, however, she died within a month of birth and was never named.

Reckless was said to be a good mother who raised well-behaved offsprings, all of whom lived with her for extended periods. Fearless was sold off the base at a young age, and nothing further was ever heard about him. Chesty and Dauntless grew up to be riding horses at the base stables. Chesty died at age 12 in 1976, while Dauntless lived to a ripe old age, although how old remains a question. In 1986, the stables held a dispersal sale and a local farrier bought Dauntless, then age 27. Hopefully the old horse enjoyed a few more years in private retirement. Both Fearless and Dauntless were given rank; whether Chesty was, as well, is not known.

In the late 1950s, Reckless left her private stable and moved, with her growing family, to the base stables. Whether too many visits to the general's hacienda played into the decision, the realization that she needed larger quarters was probably the main reason. Once there, in her own private pasture with her foals, it was also clear that there were many more people to pay attention to her—and that most certainly included all the horse-crazy children of base personnel. They brushed her, braided her mane, shared their snacks with her, and in every way they could, put her at the center of their time at the stable. Reckless ate it up.

———— 3 ————

In Marine jargon, on August 31, 1959, Reckless got her rocker. Below her chevrons, she now wore a curved bar—the rocker—that indicated the rank of staff sergeant. She was promoted by none other than her old friend, General Randolph McCall Pate, at that time the 21st Commandant of the Marine Corps. It was an incredible tribute to Reckless, indicative of the continuing esteem in which she was held by the Marines and, personally, by Pate. He had promoted her to sergeant in Korea and, in an unparalleled gesture, he was on hand again.

Her youngest son, Dauntless, had been enlisted into the Marine Corps two months earlier. Now, standing beside his mother on this August day, he, too, was promoted by General Pate, who pinned the chevron of private first class on his sheet. His older brother, Fearless, had attained the same rank two years previously, on June 12. Both followed in the footsteps of their mother as members of the Fifth Regiment.

After a 19-gun salute honoring the commandant, commanders of Camp Pendleton, the First Marine Division, and the Fifth Regiment, as well as Sergeant McLaughlin, watched more than 1,700 Fifth Marines and the First Division's drum and bugle corps parade in review. Reckless and Dauntless also looked on. The ceremonies had been opened to the public and among those in attendance were 125 Girl Scouts from the Pendleton area who, in the previous month, had made Reckless an honorary scout.

The letter accompanying Reckless' promotion warrant said in part:

"... during the period since last promotion, you have demonstrated exceptional, noteworthy and commendatory performance on unusual assignments. You participated in two 100-mile hikes with the 5th Marines ... a distinguishing observation in the January hike was the fact that you completed the event without the aid of shoes—all other participants wore field boots."

Reckless' performance of duty, as indicated by an exceptional degree of ability or qualification, merited accelerated promotion over other qualified Marines in the same occupational field, the letter also stated.

Holding the formal document, one of the commanders read the warrant authorizing Reckless' promotion to staff sergeant. Then General Pate stepped from the platform to pin the chevrons with rocker on her elaborately decorated sheet, with that signaling her advancement to staff non-commissioned officer, grade E6.

The day before they had practiced for hours, hundreds of Marines standing in formation on the parade field while, on the opposite side, Reckless waited as people talked over a microphone about how the actual ceremony would go. Perry Broughton, then a 19-year-old private, could not fathom why he had to be there, turned out with back rifle and helmet in the blistering sun.

"I'm standing there, and these people are talking about a horse. I'm thinking, 'What is wrong with this?,'" he said. It was the start of him finding out that you didn't mess around where the regiment's warhorse was concerned.

Broughton had wanted to be a Marine as long as he could remember. His uncle Glen served in World War II, his brother in the Korean War, and he enlisted right out of high school, in Peoria, Illinois, in 1958. Looking back after 22 years in the Corps, Master Sergeant Broughton could laugh at his foolishness, but soberly acknowledged the lesson he learned about respect. That, however, came after he decided to skip Reckless' promotion ceremony.

That morning, Broughton had a dental appointment, after which his clearest thought was, "I'm not going back down there and stand while they do this thing with this horse. So, I went to the library. And when I was sure they had left, I went back to the barracks." There, later in the day, his platoon sergeant caught up with him. They knew his dental appointment was early, and they had sent a runner from the parade grounds to find out what time he had left the dentist.

"Oh, boy, I messed up," Broughton recalled. "And that's when the sergeant introduced me to the term, missing the movement. They frown very seriously on that." His punishment was four consecutive days of fire watch, patrolling the company barracks in Camp Margarita. After five years at Pendleton, Reckless was still revered by the Corps for the difference her presence made in Korea, and he had shown disrespect for that. Indeed, as Broughton came to appreciate her, his tribute was as solid as any she received. Citing the Corps' first motto, *fortitudine (with fortitude)*, he described her as "standing up and doing what has to be done in the face of great peril," adding, "And you have to respect that. Even if you were a dimwitted Marine Corps private, you should have known better. He chuckled, "I've learned over the years."

———— 4 ————

Reckless rarely lacked for company. In the years she was at Pendleton, thousands came to visit her—when she was at Camp Margarita near Regimental Headquarters, and later at the base stables. Some were new friends stationed at the base, others were her old buddies who would visit when they were in the area, or travel especially to see her, bringing wives and children to meet the horse that had done so much to help the Marines. They brought treats and stayed to reminisce. The families thought she was pretty, the guys knew she was so much more.

One of them, Sergeant John Lisenby, an Arkansan who took charge of the Recoilless Rifle Platoon when Joe Latham went home in October 1953, and with it the care of Reckless, now brought his children to ride at the stables. Remembering his first reaction when, as a section leader for the rifles, he found out he would be working with a horse, he laughed, "I didn't know quite how to take that," then added, "But she sure did make a difference." It pleased him to see her life of luxury at Pendleton. "Oh, she was up to her belly in clover and hay down there. She had it made."

"If you had a Marine Corps uniform on, you know, just a plain old green one, and you talked to her, she'd come right over to the fence," said Major Butch Goewey, of Beaverton, Oregon. "She seemed to know the Fifth Marines were hers," adding, "She would be happy as could be when someone would stop and give her a treat."

In Korea, with Baker Company, First Battalion, Fifth Regiment, he had only a passing acquaintance with Reckless, but stationed at Pendleton on and off in 27 years with the Corps, he visited and was among those who brought his family to meet her. What she had done in wartime did not mean anything to his young children, he admitted, but years later his grown daughter remembered "the cute little horse that dad was so proud of."

On November 10, 1960, appropriately the Marine Corps birthday, Staff Sergeant Reckless was retired from active duty with pomp and ceremony, by order of General David M. Shoup, who succeeded General Pate as Commandant of the Marine Corps. In his letter authorizing the retirement, Shoup said:

"Staff Sergeant Reckless will be provided quarters and messing at the Camp Pendleton stables in lieu of retired pay." Standing with the same composure she showed whenever it was called for, Reckless again watched the Fifth Regiment, and the First Division's drum and bugle corps, parade in her honor around the Camp Margarita parade field. On the ground beside her handler, and out of her reach for the time being, was her first bag of oats as a retired Marine.

It was her parting gesture that Sergeant Robert Scanlon never forgot. Also from Norwalk, Connecticut, and a high school friend of Bill Bleeks, Scanlon was standing with the Fifth's First Battalion on the parade ground that day, as Reckless' handler walked her all the way around in front of the troops, one last time. "At the end of the line, just as she was exiting the grounds, she stopped," said Scanlon. "Put her head up and let out one great, big whinny, like she was saying, 'Well, thanks a lot. See you, guys.' It was fantastic."

In a manner of speaking, Reckless was handing over her ace of spades. It was her way of adhering to a time-honored tradition. Starting with a full deck of playing cards, the soon-to-be retiree throws one away every day until, driving out the main gate for the last time, the Marine leaves the ace of spades with the Military Police on duty. "That was her last card," said Larry Ames. "She was saying, 'I'm out of here.'" So typical of Marines, he maintained, "They all do something. That's a big day, no matter what. Oh, she was very traditional."

Life did not change much with retirement. Reckless no longer marched ahead of her regiment when they came back to camp after a long hike, but she still enjoyed appearances at the rodeos and the attention it brought her. She had her two last foals and, with age, was bothered by arthritis in her back. Yet her pleasure in visitors bearing treats stayed strong. Even as Korea must have been a dimming memory, her old buddies still came around, and the youngsters at the stables never stopped showering their special horse with attention.

May 13, 1968, was a warm, breezy day and Reckless, as always, was out in her private paddock. Somehow, she got tangled in barbed wire and, unable to free herself, lost her balance and fell. Still continuing to struggle, as horses will do, the barbs tore into her flesh. Help came quickly, but she had already hurt herself terribly, and lost a great deal of blood. And sadly, she could no longer get back on her feet.

The wisdom of caring Marines and horsemen prevailed and she was let go quickly, without undue debate over what could have only been an arduous and questionable recovery. The great Reckless was put to sleep with compassion and gratefulness for a life well lived. The death certification issued by the Fallbrook Veterinary Hospital, near the base, noted: "With no hope of a satisfactory recovery from her wounds and condition she was gently euthanized." She was 19 years old and was buried that day behind the base stables. A newspaper headline said it well, "Marine Mascot Ends Final Tour," followed by the lead, "Thousands of Marines the world over lost a friend ..."

Three years later, Marines came from near and far to honor Reckless with a memorial service and dedication at Camp Pendleton. It was a drizzly morning, wrote George Waselinko of November 20, 1971, when he and three other Korean War veterans drove from Encino, California. Though he had not served with Reckless, Waselinko felt it was a privilege, as a member of the First Marine Division, to be honoring her that day. In all, about 50 people gathered for the ceremony.

There was music by the First Marine Division band, the presentation of colors, and introduction of guests including Captain Pedersen, by then retired from the Marine Corps, who saw that special something in Reckless so long ago, and George Putnam, World War II Marine and popular Los Angeles commentator, who emceed the program. The Pedersens, who came from Sacramento, had not been involved with Reckless since the year she boarded with them.

The guest speaker, Lieutenant General Edward Snedeker, also retired from the Corps, had commanded the First Marine Division when their warhorse was promoted to staff sergeant. Following him, Mrs. John T. Selden, the widow of the general who first welcomed Reckless to Camp Pendleton, unveiled the memorial monument. Gladys Glover Selden had been charmed by Reckless at their first meeting and, no doubt with the passage of years, she had come to remember with a smile Reckless' recurring visits to her flower beds at the hacienda.

The monument in front of what is now the Stepp Stables is the size of a large, upright grave marker, carved of dark stone, set on a light-colored base. The bronze plaque reads, in part:

IN MEMORY OF

RECKLESS

PRIDE OF THE MARINES

KOREA

July 1949 - May 1968

Pictured above the plaque is Reckless in the new sheet she first wore in San Francisco, during those extraordinary two days after she arrived in the United States.

Sixteen years had passed since she first joined the Recoilless Rifle Platoon in the northwest corner of South Korea, interrupting a softball game in reserve camp, a few miles behind the front line. Why, someone was asked, did so many show up that many years later, some of them driving long distances to be at Reckless' memorial? The answer was simple: "She was one of us, a Marine. Semper Fi."

EPILOGUE

I first heard about Reckless from Charlie Murphy in 1992. He worked for the New York Racing Association, a real racetracker, I thought. He was a Mutuel Clerk, worked for a Chicago scratch sheet, and he knew everybody. At the time, I was freelancing for *Thoroughbred Record* magazine and hanging around Aqueduct and Belmont racetracks in New York.

Murphy seemed to have an affinity for writers. Most days, he would come up to the press box, just to see what we were doing. No matter what story I was working on, he would have a tip, something to check out that I hadn't even thought about. His widow, June, told me recently that he had been a writer himself, which explained a lot.

When he told me about Reckless, I was captivated, totally. I ran a notice in *Leatherneck*, and no sooner had the magazine come out than I heard from Katherine Pedersen. Her husband had died the year before, and she was eager to talk about Reckless, which we did a few times that spring. There had been a movie in the works with John Wayne as Lieutenant Pedersen, and Vic Damone as Sergeant Latham. Then Wayne died, and the project went with him.

Others called then. And photos began arriving in the mail. They were priceless snapshots, the Kodacolor a little faded, but there they were, the guys and their horse. Just when Charlie Murphy met Reckless, I'm not sure. He had enlisted in the Marines in World War II, then came back in for the Korean War. He stayed stateside at Marine Corps Air Station El Toro but, post war, he must have been down at Camp Pendleton at some point and, horse lover that he was, he would have found Reckless. The same as she did with everyone, she made an indelible impression. Eventually he succeeded in getting a race named for her—The Reckless, run at Aqueduct Raceway on Nov. 10, 1989.

He also thought Reckless should be in the Racing Hall of Fame at Saratoga Springs, because a note from Captain Pedersen to him in the spring of 1990 indicated that Pedersen had some documents that might help. Nothing more happened, but we know that two "old foxhole buddies"—Pedersen's name for Murphy, as one who served his country—were trying to keep Reckless' star bright.

As for me, I always knew I would write her story. But just as surely, I knew it wasn't her story alone—but their story, Reckless and her Marines. It was an amazing combination, and nothing less could have led to what occurred. It took time to find as many of her buddies as I did—more than 60 of them—but as I talked with them all, I knew my initial reaction was correct.

Reckless stayed in my back pocket, and in the file on my desk—the early interviews, piles of press clippings and news releases from the public affairs offices at Camp Pendleton and Marine Corps Base Quantico. But big projects get sidelined sometimes, and it took a while to get back to her. Then, it was like the dam burst.

I ran more notices, in *Leatherneck* and other Marine publications, and the phone started ringing. "I just got my issue. You want to talk about Reckless? I'll tell you about her." I still get a lump in my throat. The war stunk and the guys never talked about it much. But this horse stayed with them—all those years later, she was still in their thoughts. They talked for hours, some of them; sent more photos, and told me to call their buddies.

In the summer of 2013, a statue of Reckless was installed at the National Museum of the Marine Corps in Virginia. A huge crowd turned out for the dedication and, in its midst, a number of the men who had served with her had come to pay their respects. That says a lot. Reckless had that hold on the guys, and it's still there. She loved them and they loved her.

I never let her story go, either, though I'm not sure I have ever fully figured out what her hold on me is. She came with the best of the raw material—she was smarter, steadier, more sensitive, more yielding than a whole lot of horses. But that wouldn't have meant much if she and her Marines hadn't achieved the bond that they did, each allowing the other the access that made for an extraordinary partnership. As long as she was with her guys, she was ready for whatever lay ahead. In her way, she helped them feel the same.

NOTES AND SOURCES

In the long course of researching and writing this book, I consulted a myriad of sources, from histories of the Korean War and, more specifically, the part played by the U.S. Marines in that war; to magazines, newspapers, and piles of news releases and clippings from the public affairs offices at Marine Corps bases Camp Pendleton and Quantico; to websites far more numerous than I can count; to letters and photographs from those who knew Reckless.

Ultimately, it was my interviews with those who remember her that shaped the story of this warhorse and her Marines, and the events surrounding them. These people were incredibly generous with their time, a number of them talking with me repeatedly, sharing stories, and helping me to understand situations for which I had little personal appreciation. Many of them are cited directly in the chapters; all helped to inform the book. Their names are at the end of this section.

A selected list of resources follows.

Books

Ballenger, Lee. *The Outpost War: U.S. Marines in Korea, Vol. 1: 1952.* Washington, D.C.: Brassey's, 2000.

Ballenger, Lee. *The Final Crucible: U.S. Marines in Korea, Vol. 2: 1953.* Washington, D.C.: Potomac Books, 2001.

Blair, Clay. *The Forgotten War: America in Korea, 1950-1953.* New York: Time Books, 1987.

Brady, James. *The Coldest War: A Memoir of Korea.* New York: St. Martin's Press, 1990.

Cummings, Bruce. *The Korean War: A History.* New York: Modern Library, 2011.

Dant, Jack R. with Roger McGovern. *The Way of the Seahorse.* Rancho Mirage, California: Harbor House (West), 1991.

Drury, Bob, and Tom Clavin. *The Last Stand of Fox Company: A True Story of U.S. Marines in Combat.* New York: Atlantic Monthly Press, 2009.

Geer, Andrew. *Reckless Pride of the Marines.*
New York: E.P. Dutton, 1955.

Halberstam, David. *The Coldest Winter: America and the Korean War.*
New York: Hyperion, 2007.

Hastings, Max. *The Korean War.* New York: Simon and Schuster, 1987.

MacGregor-Morris, Pamela, ed. *The Book of the Horse.* New York: Exeter, 1982.

Russ, Martin. *The Last Parallel: A Marine's War Journal.* First published
by Rinehart & Company, 1957. New York: Fromm International, 1999.

Seth-Smith, Michael, ed. *The Horse. London:* Octopus Books, 1979.

Government Publications

Meid, Lt. Col. Pat, USMCR, and Maj. James M. Yingling, USMC. *U.S. Marine
Operations in Korea, 1950-1953, Vol. 5--Operations in West Korea.*
Digitized by www.mcu.usmc.mil/historydivision/, 1972.

Nalty, Bernard C. Stalemate: *U.S. Marines from Bunker Hill to the Hook.*
Washington, D.C.: U.S. Marine Corps Historical Center, 2001.

Nalty, Bernard C. *Outpost War: U.S. Marines from the Nevada Battles to the
Armistice.* Washington, D.C.: U.S. Marine Corps Historical Center, 2002.

Simmons, Brig. Gen. Edwin H., USMCR. *Over The Seawall: U.S. Marines
at Inchon.* Washington, D.C.: U.S. Marine Corps Historical Center, 2000.

Newspapers and Periodicals

Leatherneck, Magazine of the Marines.

The Old Breed News, The Official Publication of the First Marine
Division Association.

San Francisco Chronicle. "Sgt. Reckless, Famed Korean Filly, Arrives." p. 22,
Nov. 11, 1954. Microfilm from California State Library, Sacramento, CA.

Johnson, Ronald. "Marine Sergeant Reckless Lands Here -- On All 4 [sic]".
San Francisco Examiner. p. 19, Nov. 11, 1954. Microfilm from California State
Library, Sacramento, CA.

Graybeards, Magazine of the Korean War Veterans Association.

Semper Fi, Magazine of the Marine Corps League.

Website Resources

American Merchant Marine at War.
www.usmm.org

Bevin Alexander, Military History website.
http://bevinalexander.com/korea/

Canfield, Bruce, field editor. *Garand vs. Pedersen.*
www.AmericanRifleman.org

Horse Racing in Korea. *Korea Racing Blog.*
www.korearacing.wordpress.com/

Hurricane Archive: Weather Underground. Western Pacific, Eastern Pacific,
Oct.-Nov. 1954. www.wunderground.com/hurricane/wp195426.asp

Koreana, A Quarterly on Korean Art & Culture. In Search of the Jeju Horse.
www.koreana.or.kr/months/news

Korean War Educator.
www.koreanwar-educator.org

The Korean War Project. *Command Diaries 1950-1953, U.S. Marine Corps,
Fifth Regiment.* www.koreanwar.org

National Archives/Korean War Records.
www.archives.gov/research/military/korean-war/index.html

Neff, Robert. Articles on Korean history and the Jeju ponies. *The Korea Times.*
www.koreatimes.co.kr

Perry Castaneda Library. Map Collection. Army Map Service Topographical
Map Series. University of Texas at Austin. www.lib.utexas.edu/maps/korea.html

Stars and Stripes. Pacific Edition, 1950-1953. Electronic archive service:
www.stripes.com/customer-service/archives. (Also portions available at
The Library of Congress and the New York Public Library.)

U.S. Marine Corps website. www.marines.com;
www.marines.com/history-heritage/timeline

U.S. Army Quartermaster Foundation.
www.qmfund.com/horse.htm#Lessons_Learned_in_Korea

YouTube Video of racing at Jeju Race Park, South Korea
www.youtube.com/watch?v=MF7hPAwR_EA&feature.related

Personal Interviews

Benny Almonte	Debbie McCain
Larry Ames	Timothy McClure
Charles Batherson	Harold McKenna
Roland Bergstrom	Donald Menzies
Ralph Bleeks	Frank Metersky
Perry Broughton	John Meyers
James Burneson	Robert Miller, DVM
Marion Carcinieri	John Moore
Douglas Christopherson	Robert Morrisey
Maureen Shannon Cloney	Charlie Murphy
Loy Conley	June (Mrs. Charlie) Murphy
James Curtis	Blaine Myers
Donald Denny	Jack Nelmark
James Flannigan	John Newsom
Benis Frank	Paul Oshirak
Virgil Goewey	Nancy Latham Parkin
Joseph Gordon	Katherine Pedersen
Edward Guido	Louis Pelosi
John Gustafson	Howard "Jack" Railo
Paul Hammersley	Dan Richard
David Harwood	Joseph Roy
John Henkel	Robert Scanlon
Julian "Pete" Kitral	Quentin Seidel
Floyd Kummala	Gerald Smigiel
James Larkin	Joseph Stearns
Joseph Latham	Wallace Stewart
Michael Lavaia	Harold Wadley
John Lisenby	Guy Frank Wagoner
John Mailhes	J.R. Willcot
Mark Marquette	Earl Witcraft
Michael Mason, Sr.	

ACKNOWLEDGMENTS

Thank you to all those who knew Reckless, for coming forward to talk. Your names are listed under Notes and Sources. Your input every step of the way was invaluable to the success of this book.

Angele McGrady, Gordon and Audrey Ramsay, Joseph Brockbank, Mar'Kel Harkness, and Annette Erick, my editors, thank you for your wise counsel and encouragement, as the story developed.

Colonel Walter Ford, USMC (Ret.) of *Leatherneck*; Arthur Sharp, of *The Old Breed News* and *Graybeards*; and William Hudgins of *Semper Fi*, thank you for starting the ball rolling. John Lockie, thank you for your help at the Marines' Memorial Association.

Linda Fox, head librarian, and staff, Pam Larson, Patti Petrus, and Leigh Basilone, at the Chester (Connecticut) Library, thank you for your enthusiasm, and aid in moving me through sticking points.

Alisa Whitley, archivist at the Marine Corps Archives, thank you for keeping Reckless and me on your radar screen, and for the stream of information and resources that came forth.

Alastair Middleton, writer of the *Korea Racing Blog*, thank you for sharing your knowledge about racing in Korea, especially in times gone by. Ronald Pasin, thank you for your research assist.

Lynn Goodman and Sharon FitzGerald, thank you for reading the finished manuscript and giving me a final thumbs up.

Deni Auclair, thank you for your support at every step. Jess Maghan, thank you for being a special friend and mentor.

My husband, Walter, you have lived with Reckless a long time. Thank you for always believing in this book, and me.

ABOUT THE AUTHOR

Janet Barrett is the author of *On The Fence: A Parent's Handbook of Horseback Riding*. She has loved and been fascinated by horses all her life, and for 25 years almost obsessively rode, owned, and cared for them. For a time, her company, Horses For Courses, booked horses for print and TV ads.

She has written about health, sports, and education, and the people therein for a host of specialty publications, first as a staff writer and later through her own company. As well, she has written for TV, radio, and the public relations field. Barrett also operates Designed 4 Paws, creating clothes and accessories for dogs, and items for the folks who love them. She was raised in New York, graduated from Indiana University with a B.S. in Communications, and now lives with her husband in Connecticut.

NOTES ON PRODUCTION

This book was printed by Phoenix Press using electricity generated by wind. The company's Northwind 100 turbine, located on site in New Haven, Connecticut, harnesses coastal winds ranging from a low of six mph to a high of 55 mph, to produce power that enables the plant to operate with clean, renewable energy.

Marilena and Sandy Vaccaro, designers of this book, own Smart Graphics in Chester, Connecticut.